make-it-simple
entertaining
Fabulous Menus for Festive Celebrations

Nestlé Brands Appearing in This Cookbook

After Eight®
Albers®
Arrowhead®
Café Sarks™
Carnation®
Carnation® Coffee-mate®
Contadina® Dalla Casa Buitoni™
Crosse & Blackwell®
Hills Bros.®
Kern's®
Libby's®
Libby's® Juicy Juice®
Maggi®
MJB®
Nestea®
Nestlé® Baby Ruth®
Nestlé® BonBons®
Nestlé® Butterfinger®
Nestlé® Crunch®
Nestlé® Goobers®
Nestlé® Quik®
Nestlé® Raisinets®
Nestlé® Toll House®
Nestlé® Turtles®
Ortega®
Perrier®
Perugina® Baci®
Stouffer's®
Taffy Tarts®
Taster's Choice®
Willy Wonka's® Dweebs®
Willy Wonka's® Runts®
Willy Wonka's® Tart n Tinys®

A Note from Nestlé...

Welcome to Make-It-Simple Entertaining. This cookbook is about just that—making entertaining simple by providing creative menus and easy recipes. Whether you are hosting an informal birthday party or a traditional holiday meal, and working within a budget or splurging, we want to ensure your success each and every time you entertain.

Opening up your home to others and sharing your love for food is what entertaining is all about. It's energy, creativity and good food that make the event a success. With this collection of menus, we hope you discover that you can easily entertain elegantly anywhere—from your backyard to the formal dining room. All it takes is imagination and some planning. Many of our recipes can be prepared in advance so that you can enjoy more time with your family and friends.

From Our Kitchen to Yours

All of the recipes found in this book have been carefully developed and tested by our team of food experts in the Nestlé Test Kitchen and feature many tried-and-true Nestlé products. In fact, many of the ingredients called for in the recipes are probably on hand in your pantry right now!

With a rich heritage that began in 1867, Nestlé has been making products of the highest quality for families around the world. Some of Nestlé's well-known brands in the U.S. that are featured in this cookbook include Nestlé Toll House, Stouffer's, Libby's, Carnation, Contadina, Taster's Choice, Kern's and Ortega. You can be sure that all of these products come with a promise from Nestlé to be the very best in quality, great taste, convenience and value.

We're pleased to present this festive collection of menus to help make your entertaining a simple pleasure. Enjoy!

Nestlé

4

7

35

57

79

make-it-simple entertaining
table of contents

good times in the making   4 - 6

*Whether you're hosting a festive party or a casual get-together
with friends, count on these helpful planning tips from the
Nestlé Test Kitchen.*

spread the holiday cheer   7 - 34

Home for Thanksgiving ....8 - 13
Holiday Cookie Exchange ....14 - 19
Tree Trimming Open House ....20 - 23
Christmas Eve Soup Supper ....24 - 27
Hanukkah Traditions ....28 - 31
New Year's Eve Nibbles and Cheer ....32 - 34

occasions to celebrate   35 - 56

Kickoff Party ....36 - 39
Easter Basket Breakfast ....40 - 43
Wedding Shower Garden Lunch ....44 - 47
Stars and Stripes Picnic ....48 - 51
Ghosts and Goblins Party ....52 - 56

special-day fare   57 - 78

Candlelight Romance ....58 - 63
Kids' Pizza Party ....64 - 67
Fiesta con Amigos ....68 - 71
Celebration of Chocolate ....72 - 78

casual gatherings   79 - 94

Neighborhood Potluck ....80 - 83
Mix-and-Match Pasta Buffet ....84 - 87
Wine and Cheese Party ....88 - 91
Friendly Fireside Dinner ....92 - 94

index   95 - 96

Pictured on cover: Poached Salmon with Four Cheese Sauce (see recipe, page 61)

Produced by Meredith Custom Publishing, 1912 Grand Ave., Des Moines, Iowa 50309-3379.
Canadian BN 12348 2887 RT. Printed in the U.S.A.

good times in the making

Original Nestlé Toll House Chocolate Chip Cookies (see recipe, page 16), Hills Bros. Colombian Coffee with Carnation Coffee-mate

Planning a party or a special meal can be a little intimidating, but with Nestlé's *Make-It-Simple Entertaining*, you'll see how simple menus, convenience products and timesaving tips can help you host a memorable party for you and your guests.

The Best Laid Plans

Each year we look forward to celebrating our lives with family and friends whether at traditional, more formal holiday events or at more casual get-togethers such as a pizza party or a neighborhood potluck. Once you decide that you would like to entertain, draw from these ideas to put a party plan in motion:

- Consider the amount of time, money and energy you want to devote to the event. Your top priority should be to have fun, so if you're short on time or are working with a small budget, opt for a simple event. After all, it doesn't matter how lavish your party is but how enjoyable it is.
- Think about possible themes. Although a theme isn't essential for success, it can spark a festive mood

and make menu selection easier. For instance, a friendly gathering becomes a Mexican fiesta with the party menu on pages 68 through 71.

- Decide on the date, time, location and number of guests. Keep in mind how many people your home can comfortably hold and how many you can confidently serve.
- When creating a guest list, remember that the right mix of people at a party is sometimes as important as the right mix of food at your table. For formal sit-down dinners, use name cards for guest seating arrangements.
- If you plan to send invitations, send them well in advance—depending on the occasion. Make sure to write RSVP on the invitation. A phone call to friends is a personable way to invite people over for a casual gathering. If you decide to call, try to contact everyone on the same day to prevent anyone from feeling left out.

Great Food, Great Party

If you're like most hosts, you want the food at your gathering to be memorable. But that doesn't have to mean a complex menu and long hours in the kitchen. The recipes in *Make-It-Simple Entertaining* were created for busy cooks and thoroughly tested by the Nestlé Test Kitchen. Most of the recipes can be made ahead of time, which will ease your workload—and ease your mind on the big day. When choosing a menu for your get-together, consider these tips from Nestlé:

- Select menus around dishes that you feel comfortable preparing. Feel free to complement these recipes with a new recipe you have been wanting to try. You may want to test new recipes before your party so you're confident with your selections.
- Plan a menu that allows you time to join the festivities. Choose recipes that can be prepared before your guests arrive or that require minimal last-minute attention.
- Include different tastes, textures and colors in your menu. Add flair and extra flavor to main dishes with colorful chutneys and salsas or include a bright side dish such as the Firecracker Pasta Salad on page 50. Accent foods with creative garnishes, such as herbs, citrus peel curls or a sprinkling of sliced green onion.
- For casual gatherings, welcome guests into the kitchen to help with the cooking and to create an environment for easy conversation. Inviting guests to build their own tacos or decorate their own cookies can turn cooking into part of the fun.

Make a List and Check It Twice

The keys to a successful party are planning and organization. To ensure that your get-together will run smoothly and that you will stay on schedule, follow these helpful guidelines:

- Once you have selected your menu, read through the recipes, create a timetable for preparing the recipes and make a shopping list. Purchase most ingredients early in the week so you only have perishables to pick up the night before your event.
- Make a checklist of errands and of any last-minute details that you will need to attend to such as tidying up the house or purchasing flowers.
- Organize serving dishes, utensils and dinnerware several days in advance to allow time to buy or borrow pieces that you don't have. Check into renting linens, serving pieces or dinnerware for larger events.
- For sizable guest lists, keep an up-to-date tally of your RSVPs. Several days before the party, you may want to call the guests who have not responded.
- Allot a cushion of time to clean and decorate your house. This might include blowing up balloons, lighting candles and setting up a bar or area to serve beverages. Remember to try to reserve a little time for yourself to freshen up and relax.

Inviting Touches

The little extras of entertaining elevate a good party to a truly great one. These suggestions will make your guests feel pampered and will leave a lasting impression:

- For an evening event, candles add warmth, soft light and a delicate fragrance.
- Relaxing music, such as classical, provides an inviting welcome for guests. Remember to keep the volume low enough for everyone to converse comfortably.
- Welcome guests with outdoor decorations such as a wreath for Christmas, balloons for a birthday or hanging flowers for a spring gathering.
- Express yourself through a creative centerpiece such as a topiary made of dried miniature roses or a bouquet of fresh-cut flowers arranged in your favorite pitcher. Centerpieces should not be so tall or so wide that they block the view between guests.
- Personalize each place setting with a little gift or a special touch. Tie raffia bows around rolled-up napkins or place a tiny flower arrangement at each setting. A small bag of Original Nestlé Toll House Chocolate Chip Cookies, a chocolate truffle or a homemade ornament make great minigifts for each guest.

spread the holiday cheer

Home for Thanksgiving

Holiday Cookie Exchange

Tree Trimming Open House

Christmas Eve Soup Supper

Hanukkah Traditions

New Year's Eve Nibbles and Cheer

The first chilly days of winter bring on a holiday frame of mind, gearing us up for a season of celebrating. Thanks to these streamlined recipes, entertaining has never been so easy. Whether you're hosting Thanksgiving dinner or planning a festive open house, rely on these complete menus, all designed with busy holiday schedules in mind.

Home for Thanksgiving

menu

Creamy Pesto Dipping Sauce
Roast Turkey with Stuffing*
Corn Pudding
Easy Apple Cranberry Relish
Garlic Rosemary Mashed Potatoes
Bread Sticks*
Cabernet Sauvignon or Chardonnay Wir
Pumpkin Pecan Pie
Crosse & Blackwell Plum Pudding
Coffee Bar

*Prepare your favorite recipe

The time-honored foods of this American holiday are given a delectable update in this simplified Thanksgiving menu. It features all of the familiarity of the traditional autumnal feast but far less work—so you can relax and savor your dinner with family.

Clockwise from top left: Garlic Rosemary Mashed Potatoes (see recipe, page 11), Corn Pudding (see recipe, at right) and Easy Apple Cranberry Relish (see recipe, page 11)

Creamy Pesto Dipping Sauce

This incredibly indulgent dip uses only a few ingredients but packs a full-flavored punch.

⅔ cup (7 ounces) refrigerated CONTADINA
    Pesto with Basil
4 ounces cream cheese, softened

½ cup sour cream
2 tablespoons grated Parmesan cheese
  Fresh vegetables or shrimp

COMBINE pesto, cream cheese, sour cream and cheese in food processor or blender container; cover. Blend until creamy.

SERVE with fresh vegetables or shrimp. Makes 1⅔ cups.

Corn Pudding

Also called spoon bread, this Southern favorite is a pudding-like side dish, similar to a heavy soufflé. Our version uses frozen corn soufflé and muffin mix to save time.

2 packages (12 ounces *each*) STOUFFER'S
    Corn Soufflé, defrosted*
1 package (8½ ounces) corn muffin mix
2 eggs, lightly beaten
1 cup sour cream

1 cup (4 ounces) shredded cheddar
    cheese, *divided*
½ teaspoon salt
¼ teaspoon ground black pepper
¼ teaspoon garlic powder

COMBINE corn soufflé, muffin mix, eggs, sour cream, ½ *cup* cheese, salt, pepper and garlic powder in medium bowl. Pour into lightly greased 8-inch-square baking pan or 2-quart-round baking dish. Sprinkle with *remaining* cheese.

BAKE in preheated 350° F. oven for 55 to 65 minutes or until knife inserted in center comes out slightly wet (corn pudding will appear wet). Makes 8 to 10 servings.

*TO DEFROST: Remove tray from outer carton; remove film. Microwave on MEDIUM (50%) power for 6 to 7 minutes.

Turkey Roasting Guide

Take the guesswork out of preparing and roasting your Thanksgiving turkey. This helpful guide provides all of the information you'll need for roasting success:

Shopping for Your Bird
For smaller birds weighing 12 pounds or less, allow 1 pound for each serving. If the bird weighs more than 12 pounds, count on ¾ pound of turkey per serving.

Safe-Thawing Pointers
To thaw a whole frozen turkey, place wrapped frozen bird on a tray in refrigerator for 1 to 5 days, allowing 24 hours for every 5 pounds. Or, place in a sink of cold water. Change water every 30 minutes, allowing 30 minutes thawing time per pound. Do not thaw at room temperature or in warm water. Remove giblets and neck piece from cavities of thawed turkey. Rinse turkey; pat dry with paper towels. Do not stuff until roasting time.

Stuffing by the Spoonful
Spoon stuffing *loosely* into neck cavity *just before* roasting. Pull neck skin over stuffing; fasten to back with a skewer. *Loosely* spoon stuffing into body cavity. Tuck drumsticks under band of skin crossing tail or tie together with string. Twist wing tips under back.

Oven Roasting
To roast, place breast side up, on rack in a shallow pan. Place a meat thermometer into center of an inside thigh muscle so bulb does not touch bone. Cover turkey loosely with foil, leaving some space between bird and foil. Press foil over drumsticks and neck. Roast in a preheated 325° F. oven until thermometer registers 180° F. and juices run clear when a thigh is pierced with a fork. Stuffing should be at least 165° F. When turkey is two-thirds done, cut skin or string between drumsticks. Remove foil the last 30 to 45 minutes. Let turkey stand, loosely covered, for 20 minutes before carving.

Type of Turkey	Ready-to-Cook Weight	Oven Temperature	Roasting Time
Stuffed whole turkey	8 to 12 lbs.	325°	3 to 3½ hours
	12 to 14 lbs.	325°	3½ to 4 hours
	14 to 18 lbs.	325°	4 to 4¼ hours
	18 to 20 lbs.	325°	4¼ to 4¾ hours
	20 to 24 lbs.	325°	4¾ to 5¼ hours

For unstuffed turkeys of the same weight, reduce the total cooking time by 15 to 30 minutes.

Easy Apple Cranberry Relish

Combine two ready-made favorites for a sweet-and-tangy relish. The result is excellent with your Thanksgiving bird and equally as tasty with cold roasted turkey.

1 package (12 ounces) STOUFFER'S Escalloped Apples, defrosted*

1 container (12 ounces) cranberry fruit relish or 1 can (16 ounces) whole berry cranberry sauce

PLACE apples in food processor; cover. Process until coarsely chopped.

COMBINE apples and cranberry relish in medium bowl; cover. Chill for at least 1 hour. Makes about 3 cups.

*TO DEFROST: Remove tray from outer carton; cut film to vent. Microwave on MEDIUM (50%) power for 5 to 6 minutes.

Pictured on page 8.

Garlic Rosemary Mashed Potatoes

An old-fashioned comfort food with a full-flavored twist, these herbed potatoes will become a favorite year-round.

4 pounds (about 5 large) potatoes, peeled, cut into 1-inch chunks

8 cloves garlic, peeled

½ cup (2 ounces) grated Parmesan cheese

2 tablespoons butter or margarine

1 tablespoon chopped fresh rosemary or 1 teaspoon dried rosemary, crushed

1 tablespoon MAGGI Instant Chicken Bouillon

½ to ¾ cup CARNATION Evaporated Lowfat Milk Salt and ground black pepper to taste Rosemary sprigs (optional)

PLACE potatoes and garlic in large saucepan. Cover with water; bring to a boil. Cook over medium-high heat for 20 to 25 minutes or until tender. Drain.

RETURN potatoes and garlic to saucepan. Beat with hand-held mixer until combined. Add cheese, butter, rosemary and bouillon; beat until smooth. Gradually beat in evaporated milk until fluffy. Season with salt and pepper. Garnish with rosemary sprigs. Makes 10 to 12 servings.

Pictured on page 8.

Pumpkin Pecan Pie (see recipe, at right

Pumpkin Pecan Pie

For pastry leaf garnish, cut pastry scraps into leaves using knife or cookie cutter. Bake on ungreased baking sheet in preheated 350° F. oven for 12 minutes or until golden.

PUMPKIN LAYER
- 1 *unbaked* 9-inch (4-cup volume) pie shell
- 1 cup LIBBY'S Solid Pack Pumpkin
- ⅓ cup granulated sugar
- 1 egg
- 1 teaspoon pumpkin pie spice

PECAN LAYER
- ⅔ cup light corn syrup
- ½ cup granulated sugar
- 2 eggs
- 3 tablespoons butter or margarine, melted
- ½ teaspoon vanilla extract
- 1 cup pecan halves

FOR PUMPKIN LAYER:

COMBINE pumpkin, sugar, egg and pumpkin pie spice in medium bowl. Spread over bottom of pie shell.

FOR PECAN LAYER:

COMBINE corn syrup, sugar, eggs, butter and vanilla in same bowl; stir in nuts. Spoon over pumpkin layer.

BAKE in preheated 350° F. oven for 50 minutes or until knife inserted in center comes out clean. Cool on wire rack. Makes 8 servings.

coffee bar

Wind down a wonderful Thanksgiving holiday with coffee by the fire or in another cozy spot. This is easy to do with a well-dressed coffee bar, where guests can embellish their cups with a variety of finishing touches.

Coffee:
- CAFÉ SARKS Ground Coffees such as French Roast, Mocha Java and Vanilla Nut Creme

Sugar & Spice:
- CARNATION Coffee-mate Non-Dairy Flavored Creamers
- Sugar cubes or granulated raw sugar
- NESTLÉ TOLL HOUSE Semi-Sweet Chocolate Baking Bar shavings
- Cinnamon sticks
- Ground nutmeg
- Candy sticks

Flavored Liqueurs:
- Coffee
- Orange
- Hazelnut
- Almond

Bite of Sweet:
- Include a tray of bite-size treats such as AFTER EIGHT Mints, candied fruit slices, chocolate truffles and fresh berries

menu

Original Nestlé Toll House
Chocolate Chip Cookies

Lemon Bars

Pumpkin White Chip Macadamia Bars

Extra-Easy Cut-Out Cookies

Chocolate Crinkle-Top Cookies

Chocolate Eggnog

Café Sarks Gourmet Coffee

Holiday Cookie Exchange

When your holiday-season calendar is full-to-overflowing, it can be hard to find the time to continue such traditions as cookie baking and gathering with friends. Host a cookie exchange and accomplish both. Simply ask each guest to bring one recipe of cookies to share. Everyone takes home an array of holiday treats—and uplifted spirits as well.

Original Nestlé Toll House Chocolate Chip Cookies

In Massachusetts in the 1930s, a woman named Mrs. Wakefield cut a bar of Nestlé Semi-Sweet Chocolate into bits and added them to her cookie dough, expecting them to melt. Instead, the chocolate held its shape, softening to a creamy texture. The rest is history!

2¼ cups all-purpose flour
1 teaspoon baking soda
1 teaspoon salt
1 cup (2 sticks) butter, softened
¾ cup granulated sugar
¾ cup packed brown sugar

1 teaspoon vanilla extract
2 eggs
2 cups (12-ounce package) NESTLÉ TOLL HOUSE Semi-Sweet Chocolate Morsels
1 cup chopped nuts

COMBINE flour, baking soda and salt in small bowl. Beat butter, granulated sugar, brown sugar and vanilla in large mixer bowl. Add eggs one at a time, beating well after each addition. Gradually beat in flour mixture. Stir in morsels and nuts. Drop by rounded tablespoon onto ungreased baking sheets.

BAKE in preheated 375° F. oven for 9 to 11 minutes or until golden brown. Cool on baking sheets for 2 minutes; remove to wire racks to cool completely. Makes about 5 dozen cookies.

PAN COOKIE VARIATION:

PREPARE dough as above. Spread into greased 15½ x 10½-inch jelly-roll pan. Bake in preheated 375° F. oven for 20 to 25 minutes or until golden brown. Cool in pan on wire rack. Makes 4 dozen bars.

SLICE-AND-BAKE COOKIE VARIATION:

PREPARE dough as above. Divide in half; wrap in waxed paper. Chill for 1 hour or until firm. Shape each half into 15-inch log; wrap in waxed paper. Chill for 30 minutes.* Cut into ½-inch-thick slices; place on ungreased baking sheets. Bake in preheated 375° F. oven for 8 to 10 minutes or until golden brown. Cool on baking sheets for 2 minutes; remove to wire racks to cool completely. Makes 5 dozen cookies.

*May be stored in refrigerator for up to 1 week or in freezer for up to 8 weeks.

Pictured on pages 14 and 15. Also pictured on page 4.

Lemon Bars

*An all-time favorite, this two-layer bar tops a shortbread cookie base with a tangy
lemon-cream topping that just melts in your mouth.*

CRUST
- 2 cups all-purpose flour
- ½ cup powdered sugar
- 1 cup (2 sticks) butter or margarine, softened

FILLING
- 4 eggs
- 1¼ cups (14-ounce can) CARNATION Sweetened Condensed Milk
- ⅔ cup lemon juice
- 1 tablespoon all-purpose flour
- 1 teaspoon baking powder
- ¼ teaspoon salt
- 4 drops yellow food coloring (optional)
- 1 tablespoon grated lemon peel
  Powdered sugar (optional)

FOR CRUST:

COMBINE flour and sugar in medium bowl. Cut in butter with pastry blender or
two knives until mixture is crumbly. Press lightly onto bottom and halfway up sides
of ungreased 13 x 9-inch baking pan. Bake in preheated 350° F. oven for 20 minutes.

FOR FILLING:

BEAT eggs and sweetened condensed milk in large mixer bowl until fluffy. Beat in
lemon juice, flour, baking powder, salt and food coloring just until blended. Fold in
lemon peel; pour over crust.

BAKE in 350° F. oven for 20 to 25 minutes or until set and crust is brown. Cool in
pan on wire rack; chill for about 2 hours. Sprinkle with sifted powdered sugar. Cut
into bars or, for round shapes, use biscuit or cookie cutter. Makes 4 dozen bars.

Lemon Bars

Pumpkin White Chip Macadamia Bars

This moist, cake-like bar is a Test Kitchen favorite. For a more "nutty" flavor, toast the macadamia nuts before adding to the dough.

2 cups all-purpose flour
2 teaspoons ground cinnamon
1 teaspoon ground cloves
1 teaspoon baking soda
1 cup (2 sticks) butter or margarine, softened
½ cup granulated sugar
½ cup packed brown sugar

1 cup LIBBY'S Solid Pack Pumpkin
1 egg
2 teaspoons vanilla extract
2 cups (12-ounce package) NESTLÉ TOLL HOUSE Premier White Morsels, *divided*
⅔ cup coarsely chopped macadamia nuts

COMBINE flour, cinnamon, cloves and baking soda in small bowl. Beat butter, granulated sugar and brown sugar in large mixer bowl until creamy. Beat in pumpkin, egg and vanilla until blended; gradually beat in flour mixture. Stir in *1½ cups* morsels and nuts. Spread into greased 15½ x 10½-inch jelly-roll pan.

BAKE in preheated 350° F. oven for 18 to 22 minutes or until wooden pick inserted in center comes out clean. Cool in pan on wire rack.

PLACE *remaining* morsels in heavy-duty plastic bag. Microwave on MEDIUM-HIGH (70%) power for 45 seconds; knead. Microwave at additional 10-second intervals, kneading until smooth. Cut tiny corner from bag; squeeze to drizzle over bars. Makes 4 dozen bars.

Pictured on pages 14 and 15.

extra-easy cut-out cookies

The holidays just wouldn't be the same without a batch of whimsically decorated cut-out cookies. Short on time? No problem! Start with NESTLÉ TOLL HOUSE Refrigerated Sugar Cookie Dough and your favorite cookie cutters. These quick-fix cookies bake in just 7 to 10 minutes.

To decorate the cooled cookies, use purchased or homemade vanilla frosting tinted with food coloring. Liquid food coloring works well for pastel shades, while paste coloring, available in specialty stores with cake-decorating supplies, offers more vibrant colors. For a thinner, glaze-like topping, stir a small amount of light corn syrup into prepared frosting. Finish the cookies with your choice of candies or colored sugars.

Chocolate Crinkle-Top Cookies

Crisp on the outside but soft and chewy on the inside, these chocolate gems are habit-forming. The dough may be made ahead and refrigerated for up to 3 days before baking.

2 cups (12-ounce package) NESTLÉ TOLL HOUSE Semi-Sweet Chocolate Morsels, *divided*
1½ cups all-purpose flour
1½ teaspoons baking powder
¼ teaspoon salt

1 cup granulated sugar
6 tablespoons butter or margarine, softened
1½ teaspoons vanilla extract
2 eggs
½ cup powdered sugar

MICROWAVE *1 cup* morsels in medium, microwave-safe bowl on HIGH (100%) power for 1 minute; stir. Microwave at additional 10- to 20-second intervals, stirring until smooth; cool to room temperature. Combine flour, baking powder and salt in small bowl.

BEAT granulated sugar, butter and vanilla in large mixer bowl until crumbly. Beat in melted chocolate. Add eggs one at a time, beating well after each addition. Gradually beat in flour mixture. Stir in *remaining* morsels. Cover; chill just until firm. Shape dough into 1½-inch balls; roll in powdered sugar. Place on ungreased baking sheets.

BAKE in preheated 350° F. oven for 10 to 15 minutes or until sides are set but centers are still slightly soft. Cool on baking sheets for 2 minutes; remove to wire racks to cool completely. Makes about 3 dozen cookies.

Pictured on pages 14 and 15.

chocolate eggnog

Pair two best-loved holiday flavors in this stir-together treat:

COMBINE 1 quart (32 fluid ounces) refrigerated NESTLÉ QUIK Chocolate Milk and 3 cups (24 fluid ounces) prepared eggnog in large pitcher or bowl; chill. Sprinkle with ground nutmeg just before serving. Makes 8 to 10 servings.

menu

Thai Pumpkin Satay

Mini Corn Quiches

Bruschetta with Capers and Olives

Chutney Salsa with Tortilla Chips

Fudgy Caramel Brownies

Perrier Sparkling Mineral Water

*Bottom left to right: Mini Corn Quiches (see recipe, page 22), Chutney Salsa (see recipe, page 23)
Thai Pumpkin Satay (see recipe, at right) and Bruschetta with Capers and Olives (see recipe, page 22*

Tree Trimming
Open House

While you adorn the doors of your home for the holidays, invite friends in to help hang a garland or two—and to catch the spirit of this celebratory season. Greet them with a simple spread of savory and sweet treats that will fill your home with warmth and wonderful aromas.

Thai Pumpkin Satay

A popular Southeast Asian dish, "satay" means kabob and is often served with a peanut sauce. This recipe uses canned pumpkin and peanut butter to save on preparation time.

1 cup LIBBY'S Solid Pack Pumpkin
⅔ cup milk
⅓ cup creamy or chunky peanut butter
⅓ cup (about 4) chopped green onions
2 cloves garlic, peeled
2 tablespoons chopped fresh cilantro
2 tablespoons lime juice
1 tablespoon soy sauce
2 teaspoons granulated sugar

¼ teaspoon salt
⅛ to ¼ teaspoon cayenne pepper
1 pound (about 4) boneless, skinless chicken breast halves, cut into 1-inch pieces
1 large red bell pepper, cut into 1-inch pieces (about 2 cups)
2 bunches green onions, cut into 1-inch pieces (white parts only)

COMBINE pumpkin, milk, peanut butter, chopped green onions, garlic, cilantro, lime juice, soy sauce, sugar, salt and cayenne pepper in food processor or blender container. Cover; blend thoroughly. Combine ½ cup pumpkin mixture with chicken in medium bowl to marinate; cover. Chill for 1 hour.

THREAD chicken, bell pepper and green onion pieces alternately on thirty 4-inch skewers. Discard any remaining marinade. Broil 4 to 6 inches away from heat source or grill, turning once halfway through cooking time, for 10 minutes or until chicken is no longer pink in center. Heat remaining pumpkin mixture; serve with appetizers. Makes about 30 appetizer servings.

Mini Corn Quiches

Transform classic quiche into delightfully petite appetizers that are delectable when served warm from the oven.

1 package (12 ounces) STOUFFER'S Corn Soufflé, defrosted*
  Pastry for a double-crust 9-inch pie
¾ cup (3 ounces) shredded Swiss cheese, *divided*
⅓ cup chopped ham

¼ cup sour cream
1 egg
2 tablespoons chopped green onion
1 tablespoon all-purpose flour
  Sliced green onion and sour cream (optional)

CUT pastry into 2-inch squares. Place in greased mini muffin pans, pressing down to form a bottom shell.

COMBINE corn soufflé, ¼ *cup* cheese, ham, sour cream, egg, chopped green onion and flour in medium bowl; mix well. Spoon filling into shells, filling ¾ full. Sprinkle with *remaining* cheese.

BAKE in preheated 375° F. oven for 30 to 35 minutes or until golden brown. Cool in pans on wire racks for 5 minutes. Garnish with sliced green onion and a dollop of sour cream before serving. Makes 36 appetizer servings.

*TO DEFROST: Remove tray from outer carton; remove film. Microwave on MEDIUM (50%) power for 6 to 7 minutes.

Pictured on page 20.

Bruschetta with Capers and Olives

1¾ cups (14.5-ounce can) CONTADINA Recipe Ready Diced Tomatoes, drained, ⅓ *cup juice reserved*
½ cup (2¼-ounce can) sliced ripe olives, drained
2 tablespoons extra virgin olive oil
2 tablespoons CONTADINA Tomato Paste

1 tablespoon balsamic or red wine vinegar
2 cloves garlic, finely chopped
1 teaspoon CROSSE & BLACKWELL Capers
½ teaspoon salt
⅛ teaspoon crushed red pepper
1 baguette, sliced, toasted

COMBINE tomatoes and *reserved* juice, olives, oil, tomato paste, vinegar, garlic, capers, salt and crushed red pepper in medium bowl. Cover; chill for at least 3 hours.

SERVE tomato mixture on toasted baguette slices. Makes about 24 appetizer servings.

Pictured on page 20.

Chutney Salsa

A unique combination of sweet and hot makes this a refreshing and festive accompaniment to tortilla chips and grilled seafood, pork or chicken.

¾ cup chopped red bell pepper
⅔ cup canned black beans, drained
½ cup CROSSE & BLACKWELL Hot Mango or
    Major Grey's Chutney
⅓ cup whole kernel corn
2 tablespoons sliced green onion

2 tablespoons chopped fresh cilantro
1 tablespoon ORTEGA Diced Green Chiles
⅛ to ¼ teaspoon ground coriander
4 to 6 drops hot pepper sauce (optional)
    Tortilla chips

COMBINE bell pepper, beans, chutney, corn, green onion, cilantro, chiles, coriander and hot pepper sauce in medium bowl; mix well. Cover; chill for 2 hours. Let stand at room temperature for 30 minutes before serving. Serve with tortilla chips. Makes about 2 cups.

Pictured on page 20.

Fudgy Caramel Brownies

2 cups (11.5-ounce package)
    NESTLÉ TOLL HOUSE Semi-Sweet
    Chocolate Mega Morsels, *divided*
½ cup (1 stick) butter or margarine, cut
    into pieces
3 eggs
1¼ cups all-purpose flour

1 cup granulated sugar
1 teaspoon vanilla extract
¼ teaspoon baking soda
½ cup chopped nuts
12 caramels, unwrapped
1 tablespoon milk

MELT *1 cup* morsels and butter in large, heavy-duty saucepan over low heat, stirring constantly, until smooth. Remove from heat; stir in eggs. Add flour, sugar, vanilla and baking soda; stir well. Spread batter into greased 13 x 9-inch baking pan; sprinkle with *remaining* morsels and nuts.

BAKE in preheated 350° F. oven for 20 to 25 minutes or until wooden pick inserted in center comes out slightly sticky.

MICROWAVE caramels and milk in small, microwave-safe bowl on HIGH (100%) power for 1 minute; stir. Microwave at additional 10- to 20-second intervals; stir until smooth. Drizzle over warm brownies. Cool in pan on wire rack. Makes 2 dozen brownies.

Chicken and Wild Rice Soup and Pumpkin
Corn Muffins (see recipes, page 26)

Chicken and Wild Rice Soup

Cheddar Potato Soup

Minestrone

Pumpkin Corn Muffins

Mixed Green Salad*

Nestlé BonBons

Chenin Blanc Wine

Carnation Hot Cocoa

*Prepare your favorite recipe

Christmas Eve Soup Supper

Christmas Eve dinner is traditionally
modest, in comparison to the next
day's feast. A spread of hearty
soups—all of which can be made
ahead—warms the soul and prepares
everyone for an evening of ritual and
merriment. Round out this
memorable meal with a basket of
warm Pumpkin Corn Muffins and a
mixed green salad.

Chicken and Wild Rice Soup

Because wild rice takes about 30 minutes to cook, consider preparing it ahead.
Transfer cooked rice to a storage container and refrigerate it for up to 3 days.

 1 box (6 ounces) long-grain and wild rice mix,
      prepared according to package directions
 2 tablespoons vegetable oil
 8 ounces (about 2) boneless, skinless chicken
      breast halves, cut into bite-size pieces
 2 cups (6 ounces) sliced fresh mushrooms
 1¼ cups (1 medium) chopped onion
 2 cloves garlic, finely chopped
 3½ cups water

 2 tablespoons dry white wine
 4 MAGGI Chicken Bouillon Cubes
 ¼ teaspoon dried tarragon, crushed
 ¼ teaspoon dried thyme, crushed
 1½ cups (12 fluid-ounce can) CARNATION
      Evaporated Milk
 2 tablespoons cornstarch
      Sliced green onion (optional)
      Red bell pepper slivers (optional)

HEAT oil in large saucepan over medium-high heat. Add chicken, mushrooms,
onion and garlic; cook for 5 to 8 minutes or until vegetables are tender.

ADD rice, water, wine, bouillon, tarragon and thyme to saucepan. Bring to a boil.
Combine small amount of evaporated milk and cornstarch in small bowl; stir until
smooth. Stir into soup mixture with remaining evaporated milk. Reduce heat to low.
Cook, stirring occasionally, for 8 to 10 minutes or until soup is thickened. Garnish
with sliced green onion and bell pepper slivers. Makes 6 to 8 servings.

Pictured on pages 24 and 25.

Pumpkin Corn Muffins

Adding pumpkin to corn muffins boosts the flavor and makes them delightfully moist.

 1¼ cups all-purpose flour
 1 cup ALBERS Yellow Corn Meal
 ⅓ cup granulated sugar
 4 teaspoons baking powder
 ½ teaspoon salt

 2 eggs
 1¼ cups LIBBY'S Solid Pack Pumpkin
 ⅓ cup milk
 ¼ cup vegetable oil

COMBINE flour, cornmeal, sugar, baking powder and salt in large bowl. Beat eggs,
pumpkin, milk and oil in medium bowl until combined. Add to flour mixture; mix
thoroughly. Spoon batter into 12 greased or paper-lined muffin cups.

BAKE in preheated 375° F. oven for 25 to 30 minutes or until wooden pick inserted
in center comes out clean. Serve warm. Makes 12 muffins.

Pictured on pages 24 and 25.

Cheddar Potato Soup

Your friends will think you spent hours over a hot stove. When word gets out about this hearty soup, you'll need more to serve. No problem, this recipe doubles easily.

1 package (11½ ounces) STOUFFER'S Potatoes Au Gratin, prepared according to package directions
1 package (10 ounces) STOUFFER'S Welsh Rarebit, defrosted*
1 cup milk

1 tablespoon chopped green onion
⅛ teaspoon ground black pepper
⅓ cup (1½ ounces) shredded cheddar cheese
¾ cup cooked fresh or drained canned crabmeat (optional)

COMBINE potatoes au gratin, Welsh rarebit, milk, green onion and pepper in medium saucepan. Bring just to a boil, stirring constantly, over medium heat.

REMOVE from heat. Add cheese; stir until melted. Serve topped with crab. Makes 4 to 6 servings.

*TO DEFROST: Remove tray from outer carton; cut film to vent. Microwave on MEDIUM (50%) power for 5 to 6 minutes.

Minestrone

This traditional Italian soup mixes pasta, beans and a colorful bounty of vegetables for a full-bodied healthful main dish.

3 slices bacon, chopped
½ cup chopped onion
1 large clove garlic, finely chopped
2½ cups (*two* 10½-ounce cans) double strength beef broth
2 cups (15-ounce can) Great Northern white beans, undrained
1½ cups water

⅔ cup (6-ounce can) CONTADINA Tomato Paste
1 teaspoon Italian herb seasoning, crushed
¼ teaspoon ground black pepper
2 cups (2 medium) sliced zucchini
1 package (10 ounces) frozen mixed vegetables
½ cup dried small macaroni
½ cup (2 ounces) grated Parmesan cheese

COOK bacon in large saucepan over medium-high heat until crispy. Add onion and garlic. Cook for 1 to 2 minutes or until onion is tender; drain. Add broth, beans and liquid, water, tomato paste, Italian herb seasoning and pepper; stir. Bring to a boil. Reduce heat to low; cook for 10 minutes.

ADD zucchini, mixed vegetables and pasta. Bring to a boil, stirring to break up vegetables. Reduce heat to low; cook for 8 to 10 minutes or until vegetables and pasta are tender. Serve with cheese. Makes 6 servings.

menu

Sweet and Tangy Cabbage Soup

Brisket with Caramelized Onion Sauce

Potato Latkes with Applesauce

Steamed Green Beans*

Star of David Chocolate Cookies

Kosher Red Wine

Coffee with powdered French Vanilla
or Hazelnut Carnation Coffee-mate

*Prepare your favorite recipe

Brisket with Caramelized Onion Sauce (see recipe, page 30), Potato Latke
(see recipe, page 31) and Sweet and Tangy Cabbage Soup (see recipe, at righ

Hanukkah
Traditions

Among the glow of candles, Jewish families and friends gather each year to celebrate Hanukkah, also known as the Festival of Lights. This eight-day holiday celebrates a battle victory that took place over 2000 years ago, giving the Jewish Maccabees religious freedom in ancient Israel. Hanukkah's traditions are many, including the foods that are served. This menu offers a sampling of traditional dishes.

Sweet and Tangy Cabbage Soup

The intense flavor combination makes this Eastern European favorite quite remarkable. It can be made the day before and gently warmed just before serving.

1 medium head cabbage, thinly sliced	1 cup (8-ounce can) CONTADINA Tomato Sauce
3¼ cups (*two* 14.5-ounce cans) CONTADINA Recipe Ready Diced Tomatoes, undrained	2 tablespoons granulated sugar
	2 tablespoons cider vinegar
2½ cups (*two* 10.5-ounce cans) double strength beef broth	1 teaspoon salt
	¼ teaspoon ground black pepper
2 cups water	⅓ cup golden raisins (optional)
1 cup (1 small) chopped onion	

COMBINE cabbage, tomatoes and juice, broth, water, onion, tomato sauce, sugar, vinegar, salt and pepper in large saucepan. Bring to a boil. Reduce heat to low. Cover; cook for 1 hour.

ADD raisins; cook for 30 minutes or until vegetables are tender. Serve hot. Makes 6 to 8 servings.

Brisket with Caramelized Onion Sauce

*This classic Jewish recipe requires long, slow cooking
to bring out the wonderful flavors and to tenderize the beef.*

1 cup water
1 cup dry red wine
⅔ cup (6-ounce can) CONTADINA Tomato Paste
2 teaspoons dried basil, crushed
2 teaspoons dried oregano, crushed
1 teaspoon salt

½ teaspoon ground black pepper
3 tablespoons olive oil
4 cups (2 large) sliced onions
2 cloves garlic, finely chopped
1 3- to 4-pound beef brisket

COMBINE water, wine, tomato paste, basil, oregano, salt and pepper in
medium bowl.

HEAT oil in large, wide ovenproof saucepan over medium-high heat. Add onions
and garlic; cook for 2 to 3 minutes or until onions are tender. Add to tomato
paste mixture.

ADD meat to saucepan; cook on each side for 3 to 4 minutes or until browned.
Place onion-tomato paste mixture over meat. Bring to a boil; cover. Cook in
preheated 350° F. oven for 3 to 4 hours or until meat is tender when tested with
fork. Serve topped with onions and juices. Makes 6 servings.

Pictured on page 28.

Potato Latkes

Because latkes stay crisp for only a short time, serve as soon as possible after cooking.

3 pounds (4 to 6 large) russet potatoes, peeled, shredded
1 cup (1 small) finely chopped onion
2 eggs, lightly beaten
¼ cup all-purpose flour
1½ to 2 teaspoons salt

1 teaspoon baking powder
½ teaspoon ground white pepper
Vegetable oil
Applesauce (optional)
Thyme sprigs (optional)

PLACE potatoes and onion in colander; let stand for 30 minutes. Press out excess moisture. Transfer to large bowl. Stir in eggs, flour, salt, baking powder and pepper.

HEAT 2 to 3 tablespoons oil in large skillet over medium-high heat. Spoon 2 tablespoons potato mixture into skillet for each latke; spread to 4-inch circles. Fry for 3 to 4 minutes on each side, pressing down slightly when turning, until golden brown and crisp. Drain on paper towels. Repeat with remaining potato mixture; add oil as needed. Keep warm. Serve with applesauce; garnish with thyme. Makes 2½ dozen latkes.

Pictured on page 28.

Star of David Chocolate Cookies

These cookies travel well as take-home goodies. Or, mail them to friends and family who can't join you in the celebration.

2 cups all-purpose flour
½ cup NESTLÉ TOLL HOUSE Baking Cocoa
¼ teaspoon salt
1 cup (2 sticks) butter or margarine, softened

1 cup powdered sugar
1 teaspoon vanilla extract
1 container (16 ounces) prepared vanilla frosting

COMBINE flour, cocoa and salt in small bowl. Beat butter, powdered sugar and vanilla in large mixer bowl until creamy. Gradually beat in cocoa mixture. Shape dough into two balls. Roll each ball of dough between two sheets waxed paper to ¼-inch thickness. Cut with 2-inch star-shaped cookie cutter. Place on ungreased baking sheets; pierce with fork.

BAKE in preheated 350° F. oven for 8 to 10 minutes or until set. Cool on baking sheets for 2 minutes; remove to wire racks to cool completely. Decorate with frosting (see tip box, page 18, for decorating tips). Makes about 3 dozen cookies.

Breaded Ravioli with Dipping Sauces

Warm Spinach Dip in a Bread Bowl

Savory Pumpkin Cheese Ball
with Pears, Apples or Crackers

Shrimp with Crosse & Blackwell
Seafood Cocktail Sauce

Sparkling Wine

Breaded Ravioli with Red Bell Pepper Cream Sauce (see recipe, at right), Savory Pumpk
Cheese Ball (see recipe, page 34) and Warm Spinach Dip in a Bread Bowl (see recipe, page 34)

New Year's Eve
Nibbles and Cheer

After a season of feasting that begins in November, this festive

collection of appetizing finger foods is a relaxing way to ring in the

New Year—and they all team temptingly with a champagne toast.

Breaded Ravioli with Dipping Sauces

These cheese-filled pasta pillows turn crispy when cooked and are a perfect
complement to these pasta sauces.

1 package (9 ounces) refrigerated
    CONTADINA Cheese Ravioli, cooked,
    rinsed and drained
½ cup CONTADINA Seasoned Bread Crumbs
½ cup (2 ounces) grated Parmesan cheese
¼ cup all-purpose flour
1 teaspoon dried basil, crushed
½ teaspoon garlic powder
3 eggs, lightly beaten

2 tablespoons butter or margarine, *divided*
2 tablespoons olive oil, *divided*
1½ cups (15-ounce container) refrigerated
    CONTADINA Marinara Sauce, warmed
1 cup (10-ounce container) refrigerated
    CONTADINA Red Bell Pepper Cream
    Sauce, warmed
    Red bell pepper stars (optional)
    Oregano sprigs (optional)

COMBINE bread crumbs, cheese, flour, basil and garlic powder in shallow bowl.

DIP ravioli in eggs; dip in bread-crumb mixture to coat. Set on tray or baking sheet.
Repeat with remaining ravioli.

HEAT *1 tablespoon* butter and *1 tablespoon* oil in medium skillet over high heat. Add
ravioli; cook on each side for 1 to 2 minutes or until golden brown and crisp.
Repeat, adding *remaining* butter and oil as needed. Serve with sauces. Garnish with
bell pepper stars and oregano sprigs. Makes about 40 appetizer servings.

Warm Spinach Dip in a Bread Bowl

Fill a hollowed-out round of bread with this irresistible dip and use the extra bread as dippers.

2 packages (9 ounces *each*) STOUFFER'S Creamed Spinach, defrosted*
1⅓ cups (about 5 ounces) shredded Swiss cheese
1 cup (8-ounce can) water chestnuts, drained, chopped

3 tablespoons grated Parmesan cheese
1 tablespoon Dijon mustard
¼ teaspoon salt (optional)
¼ teaspoon ground black pepper
1 round bread loaf (1 pound) or 3 loaves (½ pound *each*)

COMBINE spinach, Swiss cheese, water chestnuts, Parmesan cheese, mustard, salt and pepper in large bowl.

SLICE top off loaf; carefully remove soft bread from inside, leaving ½-inch shell. Cut top crust and soft bread into bite-size pieces. Spoon filling into shell; wrap loaf in foil, leaving filling exposed.

BAKE in preheated 400° F. oven for 35 to 40 minutes or until heated through. Serve warm with bread pieces for dipping. Makes 10 to 12 appetizer servings.

*TO DEFROST: Remove pouch from outer carton; pierce several times to vent. Place on microwave-safe plate. Microwave on MEDIUM (50%) power for 6 to 7 minutes.

Pictured on page 32.

Savory Pumpkin Cheese Ball

2 packages (3 ounces *each*) cream cheese, softened
¾ cup (3 ounces) shredded sharp cheddar cheese
½ cup LIBBY'S Solid Pack Pumpkin
¼ cup (1 ounce) crumbled blue cheese
2 cloves garlic, finely chopped

1 tablespoon dry sherry (optional)
½ teaspoon curry powder
¼ teaspoon salt
½ cup finely chopped pecans
1 tablespoon chopped fresh parsley
  Sliced pears, apples or crackers

COMBINE cream cheese, cheddar cheese, pumpkin, blue cheese, garlic, sherry, curry powder and salt in mixer bowl. Beat on medium speed 2 to 3 minutes or until creamy. Cover; chill 1 hour. Mix nuts and parsley in shallow dish. Shape cheese into ball; roll in nut mixture. Serve with fruit or crackers. Makes about 16 appetizer servings.

Pictured on page 32.

occasions to celebrate

Kickoff Party

Easter Basket Breakfast

Wedding Shower Garden Lunch

Stars and Stripes Picnic

Ghosts and Goblins Party

Holidays and traditional celebrations give us reason to break away from our daily routines

and share good times with loved ones. A key part of the festivities is always the food,

prepared with care in honor of the occasion. This chapter offers spirited menus for year-

round fun. Choose a few recipes to complement favorite dishes or try a complete menu.

Kickoff Party

Today's entertaining is moving toward the casual—and there's no more informal party than one where blue jeans and sweatshirts touting your favorite football team are the perfect party clothes. This menu offers plenty to cheer about: a hearty layered dip, a game-day chili-with-a-twist and handfuls of sweet snack mix to make your party a success, no matter who wins the game.

Layered Sombrero Dip

Party-goers will have something more than football to cheer about with this south-of-the-border dip. The combination of salsa, chiles and cheese is unbeatable.

1¾ cups (1-pound can) ORTEGA Refried Beans
1 cup (7-ounce can) ORTEGA Diced Green Chiles, *divided*
2 medium very ripe avocados, seeded, peeled, and mashed
1½ cups (16-ounce jar) ORTEGA Thick & Chunky Salsa, medium or mild, *divided*

¼ cup sour cream
1 cup (4 ounces) shredded cheddar cheese
½ cup (2¼-ounce can) sliced ripe olives, drained
Sliced green onions (optional)
Chopped tomatoes (optional)
Tortilla chips

COMBINE beans and ½ *cup* chiles in small bowl. Spread over bottom of 8-inch-square baking dish.

COMBINE avocados, ¼ *cup* salsa and sour cream in small bowl; blend well.

SPREAD avocado mixture over beans. Top with *remaining* salsa, cheese, *remaining* chiles, olives, green onions and tomatoes. Serve with chips. Makes 10 to 12 servings.

Layered Sombrero Dip
with Tortilla Chips

Pumpkin Chili Mexicana

Stouffer's White French Bread Pizza

Mexican Beer

Chocolate Chip Party Mix

pkin Chili Mexicana (see recipe, page 38) and Stouffer's White French Bread Pizza

Pumpkin Chili Mexicana

Here's a zesty, colorful version that brings life to an old favorite.
Add a few jalapeño slices for a fiery chili.

2 tablespoons vegetable oil
½ cup chopped onion
½ cup chopped red bell pepper
½ cup chopped green bell pepper
1 clove garlic, finely chopped
1 pound ground turkey or lean ground beef
3½ cups (*two* 14.5-ounce cans) CONTADINA Recipe Ready Diced Tomatoes, undrained
1¾ cups (15-ounce can) LIBBY'S Solid Pack Pumpkin

1¾ cups (15-ounce can) CONTADINA Tomato Sauce
1½ cups (15¼-ounce can) kidney beans, drained
½ cup (4-ounce can) ORTEGA Diced Green Chiles
½ cup whole kernel corn
1 tablespoon chili powder
1 teaspoon ground cumin
1 teaspoon salt
½ teaspoon ground black pepper
Shredded cheddar cheese, chopped green onions and sour cream (optional)

HEAT oil in large saucepan over medium-high heat. Add onion, red bell pepper, green bell pepper and garlic; cook for 5 to 7 minutes or until tender. Add meat; cook until browned. Drain.

ADD tomatoes and juice, pumpkin, tomato sauce, kidney beans, chiles, corn, chili powder, cumin, salt and pepper. Bring to a boil. Reduce heat to low; cook, covered, for 30 minutes. Serve with cheese, green onions and sour cream. Makes 6 to 8 servings.

Pictured on page 37.

Chocolate Chip Party Mix

This mixture of cereal, pretzels, peanuts and milk chocolate morsels comes together quickly to make a bet-you-can't-eat-just-one-handful tasty snack. Substitute semi-sweet chocolate or butterscotch-flavored morsels for variety.

9 cups oven-toasted corn cereal squares	1 teaspoon vanilla extract
4 cups small pretzels	½ teaspoon baking soda
1½ cups dry roasted peanuts	2 cups (11.5-ounce package)
1 cup packed light brown sugar	NESTLÉ TOLL HOUSE Milk Chocolate
½ cup (1 stick) butter or margarine	Morsels
½ cup light corn syrup	1½ cups raisins

COMBINE cereal, pretzels and nuts in large bowl. Distribute evenly between two 13 x 9-inch baking pans or one shallow roasting pan.

COMBINE brown sugar, butter and corn syrup in medium, heavy-duty saucepan. Bring to a boil, stirring constantly, over medium heat. Boil, without stirring, for 5 minutes. Remove from heat; stir in vanilla and baking soda. Pour evenly over cereal mixture; stir until coated.

BAKE in preheated 250° F. oven, stirring every 15 minutes, for 45 minutes. Cool completely in pan(s), stirring frequently to break apart mixture. Stir in morsels and raisins. Store in airtight container. Makes about 18 servings.

game plan for victory

This party menu and the chart below let you finish most of the cooking before guests arrive so you have time to cheer on your favorite team, too.

Two Days in Advance:
- Shop for groceries, including beverages.
- Organize dinnerware, serving dishes and utensils.

The Day Before:
- Prepare Pumpkin Chili Mexicana. Cool and transfer to a covered storage container; chill.
- Prepare Chocolate Chip Party Mix; store in an airtight container.

Party Day:
- Up to 2 hours before serving, prepare Layered Sombrero Dip in an attractive glass bowl (to show off the colorful layers).
- Chill beer, sodas and any other cold beverages.
- Set table.
- Prepare garnishes for chili.
- Warm up the chili and bake the French Bread Pizzas.

40

Italian Quiche (see recipe, at right), Orange Brunch Muffins (see recipe, page 42,
and Berry Banana Smoothie (see tip, page 42).

Easter Basket
Breakfast

On most days, breakfast is a hurried meal eaten on the way out of the door. On this special spring morning, slow down and gather the family for this simple holiday breakfast featuring wedges of rich quiche and fresh-baked muffins to enjoy with fruit drinks and coffee.

Italian Quiche

A small slice of this flavorful, fresh-tasting quiche is an extravagant treat. Impress family and friends any time of year with this easy recipe.

1 *unbaked* 9-inch (4-cup volume) pie shell
¼ cup (1 ounce) grated Parmesan cheese, *divided*
2 cups (16-ounce container) sour cream
3 eggs, lightly beaten
¼ teaspoon salt
¼ teaspoon ground black pepper

3 tablespoons CONTADINA Seasoned Bread Crumbs
1 tablespoon chopped fresh basil or 1 teaspoon dried basil, crushed
3 cloves garlic, finely chopped
1¾ cups (14.5-ounce can) CONTADINA Recipe Ready Diced Tomatoes, drained
¼ cup chopped ripe olives (optional)

SPRINKLE *1 tablespoon* cheese over bottom of pie shell.

WHISK sour cream, eggs, salt and pepper in medium bowl; pour into pie shell.

COMBINE *remaining* cheese, bread crumbs, basil and garlic in small bowl; sprinkle over sour cream mixture. Top with tomatoes and olives.

BAKE in preheated 350° F. oven for 50 to 60 minutes or until filling is set. Makes 8 servings.

Orange Brunch Muffins

*A kiss of fresh orange peel makes these muffins a pleasurable morning treat,
especially when served warm from the oven.*

3 cups buttermilk baking mix
¾ cup all-purpose flour
⅔ cup granulated sugar
2 eggs, lightly beaten
½ cup plain yogurt
½ cup orange juice

1 tablespoon grated orange peel
2 cups (12-ounce package)
   NESTLÉ TOLL HOUSE Premier White
   Morsels, *divided*
½ cup chopped macadamia nuts or walnuts

COMBINE baking mix, flour and sugar in large bowl. Add eggs, yogurt, orange juice and orange peel; stir just until blended. Stir in 1⅓ *cups* morsels. Spoon into 12 to 14 paper-lined muffin cups. Sprinkle with nuts.

BAKE in preheated 375° F. oven for 18 to 22 minutes or until wooden pick inserted in center comes out clean. Cool in pans for 10 minutes; remove to wire racks to cool slightly.

PLACE *remaining* morsels in heavy-duty plastic bag. Microwave on MEDIUM-HIGH (70%) power for 1 minute; knead. Microwave at additional 10- to 20-second intervals, kneading until smooth. Cut tiny corner from bag; squeeze to drizzle over muffins while still slightly warm. Serve warm. Makes 12 to 14 muffins.

Pictured on page 40.

fruity breakfast sippers

Serve these simple fruit drinks for Easter breakfast or any morning of the year.

Berry Banana Smoothie:
PLACE 2 cups cold milk, 2 envelopes CARNATION Strawberry Creme Instant Breakfast, 1 cup fresh or partially thawed unsweetened frozen strawberries or raspberries and 1 small ripe banana in blender container; cover. Blend on high speed until smooth. For a frostier smoothie, add 1 cup ice cubes; blend until crushed. Makes 4 servings.
Pictured on page 40.

Nectar Sparkler:
COMBINE two parts LIBBY'S or KERN'S Nectar (any flavor) with one part ARROWHEAD Sparkling Mountain Spring Water in large pitcher or bowl. Serve over ice.

Pumpkin Blueberry Streusel Muffins

*Add pumpkin to old-fashioned blueberry muffins for a delightful
spin on a favorite American tradition.*

2½ cups all-purpose flour
2 cups granulated sugar
1 tablespoon pumpkin pie spice
1 teaspoon baking soda
½ teaspoon salt

2 eggs
1 cup LIBBY'S Solid Pack Pumpkin
½ cup vegetable oil
1 cup fresh or frozen blueberries
Streusel Topping (recipe follows)

COMBINE flour, sugar, pumpkin pie spice, baking soda and salt in large bowl.
Combine eggs, pumpkin and oil in medium bowl; stir into flour mixture just until
moistened. Fold in blueberries. Spoon batter into 18 greased or paper-lined muffin
cups, filling ¾ full. Sprinkle with Streusel Topping.

BAKE in preheated 350° F. oven for 30 to 35 minutes or until wooden pick inserted
in center comes out clean. Cool in pans on wire racks. Makes 18 muffins.

FOR STREUSEL TOPPING:

COMBINE ⅓ cup granulated sugar, 3 tablespoons all-purpose flour and ½ teaspoon
ground cinnamon in medium bowl. Cut in 2 tablespoons butter with pastry blender
or two knives until mixture is crumbly.

menu

Cream Cheese Crab Dip with
Assorted Fresh Vegetables or Crackers

Creamy Gazpacho

Warm Ravioli Pear Salad

Chocolate Chip Fruit Tart

Blanc de Noir Sparkling Wine

Wedding Shower
Garden Lunch

The setting for this wedding

prelude—a lush green backyard

or garden in full bloom—requires

no expensive or time-consuming

preparations to make the ambience

picture-perfect. Rely on nature's

handiwork and on the ease of this

light and elegant menu to create a

most memorable event.

Cream Cheese Crab Dip

Surround this flavorful dip with a platterful of crunchy fresh vegetables and crackers. Perfect for entertaining, the dip and vegetables can be prepared a day ahead and chilled.

8 ounces (1½ cups) cooked fresh or chopped imitation crabmeat
1 package (8 ounces) cream cheese, softened
½ cup CARNATION Evaporated Milk
½ cup (2 ounces) finely chopped water chestnuts
⅓ cup (about 4) sliced green onions
½ teaspoon garlic salt
Assorted cut fresh vegetables or crackers

COMBINE crabmeat, cream cheese, evaporated milk, water chestnuts, green onions and garlic salt in small mixer bowl. Beat on low speed until thoroughly blended. Chill for at least 1 hour before serving. Serve with vegetables or crackers. Makes about 3 cups.

Creamy Gazpacho

Center your garden shower menu around this make-ahead low-calorie chilled soup, and your lunch will be ready to serve when you are.

4 cups tomato juice
3½ cups (*two* 14.5-ounce cans) CONTADINA Recipe Ready Diced Tomatoes, undrained
1½ cups (12 fluid-ounce can) CARNATION Evaporated Skimmed Milk
⅓ cup lemon juice
¼ cup olive oil
2 cloves garlic, finely chopped
1 teaspoon salt
¼ teaspoon ground black pepper
½ teaspoon hot pepper sauce
3 cups (3 medium) peeled, seeded and chopped cucumbers
1 cup chopped green bell pepper
1 cup chopped onion
Thyme sprigs, plain yogurt, cilantro, chopped cucumber, bell pepper or onion (optional)

COMBINE tomato juice, tomatoes and juice, evaporated milk, lemon juice, oil, garlic, salt, pepper and hot pepper sauce in large bowl. Ladle into blender container; cover. Blend, in batches, thoroughly.

POUR into tureen; add cucumbers, bell pepper and onion. Stir thoroughly; chill.

SERVE cold; garnish as desired. Makes 10 servings.

Pictured on pages 44 and 45.

Warm Ravioli Pear Salad

Serve this inviting warm salad, flavored with a small amount of Gorgonzola cheese, as a side dish or as an easy main dish.

2 packages (9 ounces *each*) refrigerated CONTADINA Gorgonzola Cheese & Walnut Ravioli or Four Cheese Ravioli, cooked, drained and kept warm
⅔ cup olive oil
⅓ cup balsamic or red wine vinegar
2 teaspoons dried rosemary, crushed
½ teaspoon ground cinnamon

½ teaspoon salt
18 cups torn mixed lettuce
4 cups (3 medium or *two* 29-ounce cans) cored, thinly sliced pears
½ cup chopped walnuts
½ cup (2 ounces) crumbled Gorgonzola or blue cheese

COMBINE oil, vinegar, rosemary, cinnamon and salt in small jar or plastic container; cover. Shake until blended.

COMBINE lettuce, ravioli and pears in large bowl. Add dressing; toss. Sprinkle with nuts and cheese. Makes 12 servings.

Pictured on pages 44 and 45.

Chocolate Chip Fruit Tart

Refrigerated cookie dough makes a quick and tasty crust for this dessert. Use different fruits for variety.

1 package (18 ounces) refrigerated NESTLÉ TOLL HOUSE Chocolate Chip Cookie Dough
1 package (8 ounces) cream cheese, softened
⅓ cup granulated sugar

½ teaspoon vanilla extract
1½ cups fruit (raspberries or blueberries and/or sliced kiwi, bananas, peaches or strawberries)

PRESS dough evenly into bottom and up sides of greased 9-inch fluted tart pan with removable bottom.*

BAKE in preheated 350° F. oven for 18 to 22 minutes or until edge is set and center is still slightly soft. Cool completely in pan on wire rack.

BEAT cream cheese, sugar and vanilla in small mixer bowl until smooth. Spread evenly over cooled cookie crust to within ½ inch of edge; arrange fruit as desired. Chill for 1 hour. Remove rim of pan; slice into wedges. Makes 8 to 10 servings.

*If tart pan is not available, press cookie dough onto greased baking sheet into a 9- to 10-inch circle. Bake for 14 to 18 minutes.

Stars and Stripes Picnic

menu

BBQ Chicken with Spicy Marinade

Firecracker Pasta Salad

Southwestern Biscuits

Summer Berry Brownie Torte

Nestea Lemonade Tea

What speaks more of summertime in America than an outdoor barbecue dinner and tall glasses of iced tea? This seasonal meal, featuring an eye-catching array of foods, is perfect for daily family fare and festive enough for casual outdoor entertaining.

BBQ Chicken with Spicy Marinade (see recipe, at right), Firecracker Pasta Salad (see recipe, page 50) and Southwestern Biscuits (see recipe, at right)

BBQ Chicken with Spicy Marinade

Salsa lovers will enjoy the zesty twist on this time-honored dish. The spicy marinade enhances the color and flavor of the chicken.

1½ cups (16-ounce jar) ORTEGA Thick & Chunky Salsa, medium or mild	2 tablespoons chopped fresh cilantro
½ cup red wine vinegar	1 teaspoon garlic powder
¼ cup olive oil	4 to 4½ pounds chicken parts

COMBINE salsa, vinegar, oil, cilantro and garlic powder in large bowl or heavy-duty plastic bag.

ADD chicken; toss well to coat. Cover. Chill, turning chicken occasionally, for at least 2 hours.

BARBECUE chicken, basting frequently with marinade, over hot coals for 40 to 45 minutes or until chicken is no longer pink near bone. Makes 10 to 12 servings.

Southwestern Biscuits

Chiles add zip to these moist biscuits that are best served warm from the oven. Also try serving them with Pumpkin Chili Mexicana on page 38.

2¼ cups all-purpose flour	1 egg
2 tablespoons granulated sugar	1 cup (8-ounce can) cream-style corn
1 tablespoon baking powder	½ cup (4-ounce can) ORTEGA Diced Green Chiles
3 tablespoons butter or margarine, softened	1 tablespoon chopped fresh cilantro (optional)

COMBINE flour, sugar and baking powder in large bowl. Add butter; cut in with pastry blender or two knives until mixture resembles coarse crumbs.

STIR in egg, corn, chiles and cilantro; combine just until mixture holds together. Knead dough 10 times on well-floured surface. Pat dough to ¾-inch thickness. Cut into 3-inch biscuits. Place on greased baking sheets.

BAKE in preheated 400° F. oven for 20 to 25 minutes or until wooden pick inserted in center comes out clean. Cool on baking sheets for 5 minutes; remove to wire racks to cool completely. Makes about 8 biscuits.

Firecracker Pasta Salad

This garden pasta salad is high in flavor and low in preparation time.
Make it ahead and store in the refrigerator for easy summer entertaining.

2 packages (9 ounces *each*) refrigerated
   CONTADINA Three Cheese Tortellini,
   cooked, drained and chilled
¼ cup olive oil
4 to 5 large cloves garlic, finely chopped
2 to 3 tablespoons red wine vinegar

2 cups (2 medium) chopped tomatoes
2 cups broccoli florets
1 cup (1 large) chopped green bell pepper
½ cup pitted and halved ripe olives
½ cup (2 ounces) shredded Parmesan cheese
¼ cup (1 ounce) shredded Romano cheese

HEAT oil in small saucepan over medium-high heat. Add garlic; cook for 1 minute.
Pour into large bowl; cool. Whisk in vinegar. Add pasta, tomatoes, broccoli, bell pepper,
olives and cheeses; toss well. Chill or serve immediately. Makes 8 to 10 servings.

Pictured on page 48.

Summer Berry Brownie Torte

¾ cup granulated sugar
6 tablespoons butter or margarine
1 tablespoon water
1½ cups (9 ounces) NESTLÉ TOLL HOUSE Semi-
   Sweet Chocolate Morsels, *divided*
½ teaspoon vanilla extract

2 eggs
⅔ cup all-purpose flour
¼ teaspoon baking soda
¼ teaspoon salt
   Filling (recipe follows)
2 cups sliced strawberries and blueberries

COMBINE sugar, butter and water in small, heavy-duty saucepan. Bring to a boil,
stirring constantly; remove from heat. Add ¾ *cup* morsels; stir until smooth. Stir in
vanilla. Add eggs one at a time, stirring well after each addition. Add flour, baking
soda and salt; stir until well blended. Stir in *remaining* morsels. Pour into waxed
paper-lined and greased 9-inch-round cake pan.

BAKE in preheated 350° F. oven for 20 to 25 minutes or until wooden pick inserted
in center comes out slightly sticky. Cool in pan for 15 minutes. Invert onto wire
rack; remove waxed paper. Turn right side up; cool completely. Spread Filling over
brownie; top with berries. Chill until serving time. Makes 8 to 10 servings.

FOR FILLING:
BEAT ½ cup heavy whipping cream and ¼ cup granulated sugar in small mixer bowl
until stiff peaks form.

...er Berry Brownie Torte (see recipe, at left)

Ghosts and Goblins Party

Even some of the party treats put on costumes in this kid-pleasing collection of fun Halloween foods. The specialties you serve at your ghoulish bash will thrill little ghosts and goblins even more than what's in their trick-or-treat bags—and there's a special treat for the cook: the recipes are child's play to put together.

English Muffin Pizzas

These mini party pizzas take just minutes to prepare and are so easy to make that kids can assemble their own.

6 sandwich-size English muffins, split, toasted
¾ cup CONTADINA PIZZA SQUEEZE Pizza Sauce, *divided*

4 ounces sliced pepperoni or chopped ham
½ cup chopped green or yellow bell pepper
1¼ cups (5 ounces) shredded mozzarella cheese

SPREAD each muffin half with *1 tablespoon* pizza sauce. Top muffins with pepperoni, bell pepper and cheese.

BROIL, 4 to 6 inches away from heat source, for 1 to 2 minutes or until cheese is melted. Makes 12 servings.

menu

English Muffin Pizzas

Cheesy Macaroni and Hot Dogs

Fruit Kabobs*

Spiderweb Munch

Monster Pops

Libby's Juicy Juice

*Prepare your favorite recipe

esy Macaroni and Hot Dogs (see recipe, page 54)
English Muffin Pizzas (see recipe, at left)

Cheesy Macaroni and Hot Dogs

Everyone knows macaroni and cheese is a favorite with kids; combined with hot dogs—it's a real winner.

1 package (40 ounces) STOUFFER'S Macaroni and Cheese, defrosted*	4 hot dogs, cut into ½-inch-thick slices

ADD hot dogs to macaroni and cheese in tray; place on baking sheet.

BAKE in preheated 350° F. oven for 25 to 30 minutes or until hot. Or, microwave on HIGH (100%) power for 6 minutes; stir. Microwave for an additional 6 minutes or until hot. Makes 10 servings.

*TO DEFROST: Remove tray from outer carton; cut film to vent. Microwave on MEDIUM (50%) power for 20 to 25 minutes.

Pictured on page 53.

Spiderweb Munch

Kids and adults alike will love to munch on this giant chocolaty peanut butter dessert.

2 cups (12-ounce package) NESTLÉ TOLL HOUSE Semi-Sweet Chocolate Morsels	1 cup creamy peanut butter, *divided*
	⅓ cup powdered sugar
	3 cups toasted rice cereal

HEAT morsels and ¾ *cup* peanut butter in small, heavy-duty saucepan over low heat, stirring constantly until smooth; remove from heat. Add powdered sugar; stir vigorously until smooth.

PLACE cereal in large bowl. Add 1 cup melted chocolate mixture; stir until all cereal is coated. Place on ungreased baking sheet. Using small metal spatula, shape into 10-inch circle with slightly raised 1-inch-wide border. Pour remaining melted chocolate mixture in center of circle; spread to border.

FOR SPIDERWEB:

PLACE *remaining* peanut butter in heavy-duty plastic bag. Cut tiny corner from bag; squeeze to pipe concentric circles on top of chocolate. Using wooden pick or tip of sharp knife, pull tip through peanut butter from center to border. Chill for 30 minutes or until firm. Cut into wedges to serve. Makes 12 to 16 servings.

Monster Pops

*Kids will have a field day turning these giant cookies into monster faces
with frosting and assorted Nestlé candies.*

1⅔ cups all-purpose flour
1 teaspoon baking soda
½ teaspoon salt
1 cup (2 sticks) butter or margarine, softened
¾ cup granulated sugar
¾ cup packed brown sugar
2 teaspoons vanilla extract
2 eggs
2 cups (12-ounce package)
  NESTLÉ TOLL HOUSE Semi-Sweet
  Chocolate Morsels

2 cups quick or old-fashioned oats
1 cup raisins
About 24 wooden craft sticks
1 container (16 ounces) prepared vanilla
  frosting, colored as desired, or colored
  icing in tubes
Colored candies: WILLY WONKA'S RUNTS,
  TART N TINYS and DWEEBS

COMBINE flour, baking soda and salt in small bowl. Beat butter, granulated sugar, brown sugar and vanilla in large mixer bowl until creamy. Beat in eggs. Gradually beat in flour mixture. Stir in morsels, oats and raisins. Drop dough by level ¼-cup measure 3 inches apart onto ungreased baking sheets. Shape into round mounds. Insert wooden stick into side of each mound.

BAKE in preheated 325° F. oven for 14 to 18 minutes or until golden brown. Cool on baking sheets for 2 minutes; remove to wire racks to cool completely.

DECORATE pops using colored frosting and candies. Makes about 2 dozen cookies.

Monster Pops

Tuxedo Cheesecake (see recipe, page 74)

special-day fare

Candlelight Romance

Kids' Pizza Party

Fiesta con Amigos

Celebration of Chocolate

A little celebrating goes a long way to show loved ones how much you care about their special days. Throw a spirited pizza party for a child's birthday, or recognize a recent promotion or accomplishment with a chocolate bash. To make these occasions easy on the cook, the menus feature simplified and make-ahead recipes, as well as helpful tips.

Poached Salmon with Four Cheese Sauce *(see recipe, page 61)*

menu

Cream of Pumpkin Curry Soup

Poached Salmon with Four Cheese Sauce

Steamed Asparagus and Baby Squash*

Tossed Green Salad*

Garlic Toast

Sauvignon Blanc Wine

Rich Chocolate Mocha Mousse

After Eight Mints

Taster's Choice Original Blend Freeze
Dried Coffee

Prepare your favorite recipe

Candlelight
Romance

For an evening, make the world

revolve only around a candlelit table

for two. This special dinner is an

intimate antidote for whirlwind

lives—ideal for celebrating

Valentine's Day, an anniversary or

simply for spending time together. Its

elegance treats your loved one well,

and its ease of preparation will suit

you well, too.

Cream of Pumpkin Curry Soup

The mix of pumpkin and curry makes this velvety soup an intriguing first course for a romantic evening. With the harvest-gold color, it would also make an elegant first course for Thanksgiving dinner—just double the recipe.

3 tablespoons butter
1 cup (1 small) finely chopped onion
1 clove garlic, finely chopped
1 teaspoon curry powder
½ teaspoon salt
⅛ to ¼ teaspoon ground coriander
⅛ teaspoon crushed red pepper

3 cups water
3 MAGGI Vegetarian Vegetable Bouillon Cubes
1¾ cups (15-ounce can) LIBBY'S Solid Pack Pumpkin
1 cup half-and-half
Sour cream and chopped fresh chives (optional)

MELT butter in large saucepan over medium-high heat. Add onion and garlic; cook for 3 to 5 minutes or until tender. Stir in curry powder, salt, coriander and crushed red pepper; cook for 1 minute. Add water and bouillon; bring to a boil. Reduce heat to low; cook, stirring occasionally, for 15 to 20 minutes to develop flavor. Stir in pumpkin and half-and-half; cook for 5 minutes or until heated through.

TRANSFER mixture to food processor or blender container (in batches, if necessary); cover. Blend until creamy. Serve warm or reheat to desired temperature. Garnish with a dollop of sour cream and chives. Makes 4 servings.

garlic toast

Try this quick and tasty recipe:

COMBINE 2 tablespoons softened butter, 1 tablespoon shredded Parmesan cheese and 1 finely chopped clove garlic in small bowl. Spread onto six French baguette slices.

BROIL for about 1 minute or until golden brown.

Poached Salmon with Four Cheese Sauce

Simple yet elegant, poached salmon is a dish which may be prepared for any sophisticated occasion. Try poaching twice the amount of fish and serving it the next day over mixed lettuce for a cold salmon salad.

1 package (9 ounces) refrigerated CONTADINA Linguine, cooked, drained and kept warm
1 cup (10-ounce container) refrigerated CONTADINA Four Cheese Sauce, warmed
½ cup water
¼ cup dry white wine or chicken broth

¼ teaspoon salt
⅛ teaspoon ground black pepper
2 (6 ounces *each*) salmon fillets or steaks
2 tablespoons finely grated carrot (optional)
1 tablespoon chopped fresh parsley (optional)
  Dill weed sprigs (optional)

COMBINE water, wine, salt and pepper in large skillet. Bring to a boil; add salmon. Reduce heat to low; cook, covered, for 8 to 10 minutes or until thickest part of salmon flakes easily when tested with fork.

TOSS pasta with carrot and parsley; divide onto plates. Top with salmon. Spoon sauce over each serving; garnish with dill weed. Makes 2 servings.

Pictured on the cover and on pages 58 and 59.

Rich Chocolate Mocha Mousse (see recipe, at right

Rich Chocolate Mocha Mousse

Unlike ordinary mousse, this dessert is especially rich and dense—the ultimate for chocolate lovers. Serve topped with whipped cream and piped chocolate zigzags (see tip below).

1 cup (6 ounces) NESTLÉ TOLL HOUSE Semi-Sweet Chocolate Morsels
3 tablespoons butter, cut into pieces
2 teaspoons TASTER'S CHOICE Original Blend Freeze Dried Coffee

1 tablespoon hot water
2 teaspoons vanilla extract
½ cup heavy whipping cream
Sweetened whipped cream (optional)
Chocolate Zigzags

MICROWAVE morsels and butter in medium, microwave-safe bowl on HIGH (100%) power for 1 minute; stir. Microwave at additional 10- to 20-second intervals, stirring until smooth. Dissolve coffee in hot water; stir into chocolate mixture. Stir in vanilla; cool to room temperature.

WHIP cream in small mixer bowl on high speed until stiff peaks form; fold into chocolate mixture. Spoon into tall glasses; chill for 1 hour or until set. Garnish with whipped cream and Chocolate Zigzags. Makes 2 servings.

chocolate zigzags

To make chocolate zigzags or any piped design that you desire, place about ¼ cup NESTLÉ TOLL HOUSE Semi-Sweet Chocolate Morsels in heavy-duty plastic bag. Microwave on HIGH (100%) power for about 30 seconds; knead until smooth. Cut tiny corner from bag; squeeze designs onto waxed paper. Chill until firm.

Kids' Pizza Party

menu

Nacho Pizza

Fiesta Pizza

Juicy Gelatin Salad

Candy Shop Pizza

Ice-Cream Dream Sundaes

Carnation Mini Marshmallows Rich
Chocolate Hot Cocoa

Throw the best birthday party on the block by serving up every kid's favorite food—
pizza! Two south-of-the-border pizzas, a fruity gelatin salad and a candy-topped dessert
pizza are just the right treats to make any celebration great.

64   *Nacho Pizza, Juicy Gelatin Salad (see recipes, at right) and Ice-Cream Dream Sundaes (see tip, page 66)*

Nacho Pizza

Your kids' favorites rolled into one—pizza and nachos!
Watch them go wild for a slice of this premium pizza pie!

1 12-inch prepared pizza crust	½ cup (2 ounces) shredded cheddar cheese
1 cup (*half* 14.5-ounce can) CONTADINA Chunky Pizza Sauce, Original	¼ cup sliced ripe olives, drained
¾ cup (*about half* 1-pound can) ORTEGA Refried Beans	1 tablespoon ORTEGA Diced Green Chiles
	Tortilla chips (optional)
1 cup (4 ounces) shredded mozzarella cheese	Chopped fresh cilantro (optional)

COMBINE pizza sauce and beans in small saucepan. Cook, stirring constantly, over low heat for 1 to 2 minutes or until smooth.

SPREAD sauce mixture over crust to within 1 inch of edge; top with mozzarella cheese, cheddar cheese, olives and chiles.

BAKE according to pizza crust package directions or until crust is crisp and cheese is melted. Garnish with tortilla chips and cilantro. Makes 8 servings.

Juicy Gelatin Salad

Parents like the fact that this gelatin salad uses real fruit juice, while kids are crazy
about the cherry flavor and chunks of fresh fruit.

5 cups (40 ounces) LIBBY'S Cherry Juicy Juice, *divided*	1½ cups sliced strawberries, halved red and green grapes or sliced bananas
4 envelopes (.25 ounces *each*) unflavored gelatin	Whipped cream (optional)

POUR *1 cup* juice into large bowl; sprinkle with gelatin. Pour *remaining* juice into medium saucepan; bring just to a boil over medium-high heat. Pour into bowl with gelatin; stir until gelatin is completely dissolved.

POUR into 8-inch-square baking pan. Gently stir in fruit; cool. Chill for 2 to 3 hours or until set. Garnish with whipped cream. Makes 9 to 12 servings.

Fiesta Pizza

Taco seasoning spices up the ground beef in one easy step,
and the taco taste gives party-goers another reason to celebrate.

1   12-inch prepared pizza crust
8   ounces lean ground beef
¼   cup water
2   tablespoons (*half* 1.25-ounce package)
      ORTEGA Taco Seasoning Mix
1   cup (*half* 14.5-ounce can) CONTADINA
      Chunky Pizza Sauce, Three Cheeses

1   cup (4 ounces) shredded mozzarella cheese
¼   cup sliced ripe olives, drained
¼   cup whole kernel corn
¼   cup (1 ounce) shredded cheddar cheese
2   tablespoons chopped green bell pepper

COOK beef in medium skillet over medium-high heat for 4 to 5 minutes or until no longer pink; drain. Add water and taco seasoning mix; cook for 1 minute or until most of water is evaporated.

SPREAD pizza sauce over crust to within 1 inch of edge. Top with meat mixture, mozzarella cheese, olives, corn, cheddar cheese and bell pepper.

BAKE according to pizza crust package directions or until crust is crisp and cheese is melted. Makes 8 servings.

ice-cream dream sundaes

Start scooping CARNATION ice cream into dishes and watch the kids come running. You'll see their creativity flourish with the assortment of toppings for design-your-own sundaes.

Toppings:
Drizzle NESTLÉ QUIK Real Chocolate Flavor Syrup atop ice cream right from the squeeze bottle.

Place colorful Nestlé candies, such as TAFFY TARTS, WILLY WONKA'S TART N TINYS and RUNTS and NESTLÉ GOOBERS and RAISINETS, into small bowls with spoons and let kids serve themselves.

Candy Shop Pizza

Kids will race through dinner to get to dessert once they see this candy-studded pizza—
truly a clever twist on the pizza party theme.

1 package (18 ounces) refrigerated
    NESTLÉ TOLL HOUSE Chocolate Chip
    Cookie Dough
1 cup (6 ounces) NESTLÉ TOLL HOUSE Semi-
    Sweet Chocolate Morsels

½ cup creamy or chunky peanut butter
1 cup coarsely chopped assorted candy:
    NESTLÉ CRUNCH, BUTTERFINGER, BABY
    RUTH, GOOBERS, RAISINETS

PRESS cookie dough evenly onto bottom of greased 12-inch pizza pan or
13 x 9-inch baking pan.

BAKE in preheated 350° F. oven for 14 to 18 minutes or until edge is set and center
is still slightly soft. Immediately sprinkle morsels over hot crust; drop peanut butter
by spoonfuls onto morsels. Let stand for 5 minutes or until morsels become shiny
and soft. Gently spread chocolate and peanut butter evenly over cookie crust.

SPRINKLE candy in single layer over pizza. Cut into wedges; serve warm or at room
temperature. Makes 12 servings.

menu

Taco Bar

Ortega Guacamole with Tortilla Chips

Mexican Rice

Fiesta Corn Bread

Mini Cream Cheese Flans

Margaritas

Taco Bar (see tip, page 70), Mexican Rice (see recipe, page 70), Fiesta Corn Bread (see recipe, at right) and Ortega Guacamole (see recipe, page 71

Fiesta con Amigos

You don't need a special reason to throw a casual dinner party. This Mexican-themed menu keeps the cooking simple with a little help from your friends. Welcome them into the kitchen to create their own fiesta tacos. Layering the corn shells with tasty fillings is more fun than work, and the result is plenty of time to enjoy the party yourself.

Fiesta Corn Bread

An ethnic twist on a traditional recipe, this quick bread tastes best when made the day of the fiesta. For all of you spicy-food lovers, add sliced jalapeños for extra heat. Olé!

2¼ cups all-purpose flour	2 tablespoons baking powder
1¾ cups ALBERS Corn Meal	1½ teaspoons salt
1½ cups (6 ounces) shredded cheddar cheese	2 cups milk
1 cup (7-ounce can) ORTEGA Diced Green Chiles	⅔ cup vegetable oil
½ cup granulated sugar	2 eggs, lightly beaten

COMBINE flour, cornmeal, cheese, chiles, sugar, baking powder and salt in large bowl. Add milk, oil and eggs; stir just until moistened. Spread into greased 13 x 9-inch baking pan.

BAKE in preheated 375° F. oven for 30 to 35 minutes or until wooden pick inserted in center comes out clean. Cool in pan for 10 minutes; cut into squares. Cut squares diagonally in half. Makes 24 servings.

Mexican Rice

No fiesta is complete without this colorful side dish.
For a richer flavor, substitute chicken stock for the water.

2 tablespoons butter or margarine
½ cup chopped onion
2 cloves garlic, finely chopped
1½ cups (16-ounce jar) ORTEGA Thick & Chunky
   Salsa, hot, medium or mild

1¼ cups water
¾ cup (1 large) shredded carrot
½ cup frozen peas, thawed
1 cup long-grain white rice
   Sliced fresh jalapeño (optional)

MELT butter in large saucepan over medium heat. Add onion and garlic; cook for 2 to 3 minutes or until tender. Stir in salsa, water, carrot and peas. Bring to a boil; stir in rice. Reduce heat to low; cook, covered, for 25 to 30 minutes or until liquid is absorbed and rice is tender. Garnish with jalapeño slices. Makes 8 servings.

Pictured on page 68.

taco bar

Start the party in the kitchen! Guests tend to congregate there, so invite them in to help themselves. Place a platter of ORTEGA White and Yellow Corn Taco Shells at the beginning of the bar and set out bowls filled with:

- Ground beef or turkey prepared with ORTEGA Taco Seasoning Mix
- ORTEGA Refried Beans, warmed
- Shredded lettuce
- Chopped tomatoes
- Sliced avocados
- Chopped green onions
- Sliced ripe olives
- ORTEGA Sliced Jalapeños
- Chopped fresh cilantro
- Shredded cheddar and Monterey Jack cheeses
- ORTEGA Taco Sauce

Ortega Guacamole

2 medium very ripe avocados, seeded, peeled, and mashed
⅓ cup ORTEGA Thick & Chunky Salsa, hot, medium or mild
¼ cup sour cream
2 tablespoons finely chopped onion
2 tablespoons chopped fresh cilantro

1 teaspoon lime juice
1 clove garlic, finely chopped
¼ teaspoon salt
ORTEGA Thick & Chunky Salsa, hot, medium or mild
Tortilla chips

COMBINE avocados, *⅓ cup* salsa, sour cream, onion, cilantro, lime juice, garlic and salt in medium bowl. Cover; chill for at least 1 hour. Garnish with additional salsa; serve with tortilla chips. Makes 2 cups.

Pictured on page 68.

Mini Cream Cheese Flans

1 cup granulated sugar
½ cup water
1½ cups (12 fluid-ounce can) CARNATION Evaporated Milk
1¼ cups (14-ounce can) CARNATION Sweetened Condensed Milk

1 package (8 ounces) cream cheese, softened
¼ cup (½ stick) butter, softened
5 eggs
1 teaspoon vanilla extract

FILL two 13 x 9-inch baking pans with hot water to 1-inch depth. Place twelve 6-ounce custard cups in prepared pans.

COMBINE sugar and water in small saucepan. Cook, stirring constantly, over low heat for 2 minutes or until sugar is dissolved. Bring to a boil. Boil, without stirring, for 10 to 15 minutes or until golden brown. Quickly pour evenly into custard cups.

COMBINE evaporated milk, sweetened condensed milk, cream cheese, butter, eggs and vanilla in blender container; cover. Blend until smooth. Pour into prepared cups.

BAKE in preheated 350° F. oven for 35 to 45 minutes or until knife inserted near center comes out clean. Cool in pans on wire racks for 20 minutes. Remove custard cups from baking pans; chill for several hours or overnight. Run knife around rims; shake gently to loosen. Invert onto serving dishes. Makes 12 servings.

Celebration of
Chocolate

Well suited to an after-theater

gathering, a New Year's Eve dessert

buffet, an adult birthday party—or

when you don't have time to serve a

complete dinner—these sophisticated

and surprisingly simple-to-make

sweets transform a favorite course

into a cause for celebration in itself.

*plate clockwise from top: Glazed Chocolate Sweet Cakes (see recipe,
page 75), Chocolate Cookie Turtle Shapes (see recipe, page 77) and
...ation Famous Fudge (see recipe, page 78). Mocha Cream Shake (see
..., page 77) and Luscious Chocolate Mousse Pie (see recipe, page 76)*

73

Tuxedo Cheesecake

For a showstopping dessert, try this elegant cheesecake made with white morsels and a chocolate cookie crust. To make chocolate curls, see Decorating with Chocolate, page 76.

CRUST
1¾ cups (about 18) crushed creme-filled
   chocolate cookies
2 tablespoons butter or margarine, melted

CHEESECAKE
1 cup (6 ounces) NESTLÉ TOLL HOUSE
   Premier White Morsels

3 packages (8 ounces *each*) cream cheese,
   softened
¾ cup granulated sugar
2 teaspoons vanilla extract
3 eggs
1 bar (2 ounces) NESTLÉ TOLL HOUSE Semi-
   Sweet or Premier White Baking Chocolate,
   made into curls or grated

FOR CRUST:

TOSS cookie crumbs and butter together in medium bowl. Press onto bottom of ungreased 9-inch springform pan. Bake in preheated 350° F. oven for 10 minutes.

FOR FILLING:

MICROWAVE morsels in small, microwave-safe bowl on MEDIUM-HIGH (70%) power for 1 minute; stir. Microwave at additional 10- to 20-second intervals, stirring until smooth; cool to room temperature.

BEAT cream cheese, sugar and vanilla in large mixer bowl until smooth. Beat in eggs. Gradually beat in melted white morsels. Spread over chocolate crust.

BAKE in 350° F. oven for 40 to 50 minutes or until edges are set but center still moves slightly. Cool in pan on wire rack; chill until firm. Remove side of springform pan. Garnish with chocolate curls before serving. Makes 14 to 16 servings.

Pictured on page 57.

choice cheesecakes

Cheesecakes aren't hard to make, but they do take a little special care. Follow these tips from the NESTLÉ Test Kitchen for top-notch results:

• Use a springform pan with removable side and bottom.
• For cheesecakes with a crumb crust, spray bottom and side of pan lightly with no-stick spray before adding the crumbs. This helps them stick to the pan.
• Use cream cheese that is at room temperature, but not too soft. To avoid lumps, make sure the cream cheese and sugar are thoroughly combined before adding the other ingredients.
• Be careful not to overbeat the batter, especially after the eggs have been added, to help prevent cracking after the cake is baked.

Glazed Chocolate Sweet Cakes

The shiny, dainty appearance of these minicakes makes them especially tantalizing treats. But don't be fooled—inside lies rich chocolate heaven.

CAKES
- 2 cups (12-ounce package) NESTLÉ TOLL HOUSE Semi-Sweet Chocolate Morsels, *divided*
- 1½ cups all-purpose flour
- 1 teaspoon baking soda
- 1 teaspoon salt
- ½ cup granulated sugar
- ⅓ cup vegetable oil
- 1 egg
- 1 teaspoon vanilla extract
- 1 cup water

GLAZE
- ⅔ cup heavy whipping cream
- 2 tablespoons butter or margarine
- 2 tablespoons light corn syrup
- Sweetened whipped cream (optional)
- Orange peel curls (optional)

FOR CAKES:

MICROWAVE *1 cup* morsels in small, microwave-safe bowl on HIGH (100%) power for 1 minute; stir. Microwave at additional 10- to 20-second intervals, stirring until smooth. Cool to room temperature. Combine flour, baking soda and salt in small bowl.

BEAT sugar, oil, egg and vanilla in large mixer bowl until blended. Beat in melted chocolate. Gradually beat in flour mixture alternately with water. Spoon into 12 greased muffin cups.

BAKE in preheated 350° F. oven for 18 to 22 minutes or until wooden pick inserted in center comes out clean. Let stand for 20 minutes. Remove from pan; turn upside down on wire rack to cool completely. Trim edges with scissors, if necessary.

FOR GLAZE:

HEAT *remaining* morsels, cream, butter and corn syrup in medium, heavy-duty saucepan over medium heat until mixture comes to a boil, stirring constantly. Remove from heat; stir until smooth. Cool to room temperature. Spread Glaze over sides and flat tops of Sweet Cakes or dip into Glaze. Garnish with whipped cream and orange peel curls just before serving. Makes 12 minicakes.

Pictured on pages 72 and 73.

Luscious Chocolate Mousse Pie

*This is perhaps the world's easiest chocolate pie to make—
and the most pleasing. Your guests will come back for more.*

1 8-inch (6 ounces) prepared chocolate
     crumb crust
2¼ cups (about 15 ounces) NESTLÉ TOLL
     HOUSE Semi-Sweet Chocolate Morsels,
     divided

2 cups heavy whipping cream, *divided*
2 teaspoons powdered sugar
1 teaspoon vanilla extract
     Chocolate Drizzle (directions follow)

MICROWAVE *2 cups* morsels and ¾ *cup* cream in large, microwave-safe bowl on
HIGH (100%) power for 1 minute; stir. Microwave at additional 10- to 20-second
intervals, stirring until smooth; cool to room temperature.

BEAT *remaining* cream, powdered sugar and vanilla in chilled small mixer bowl until
soft peaks form. Fold 2 cups whipped cream into chocolate mixture. Spoon into
crust; swirl top. Garnish with remaining whipped cream; chill until firm. Garnish
with Chocolate Drizzle; let stand a few minutes before serving. Makes 8 servings.

FOR CHOCOLATE DRIZZLE:
MICROWAVE *remaining* ¼ *cup* morsels in heavy-duty plastic bag on HIGH (100%)
power about 30 seconds; knead until smooth. Cut tiny corner from bag; squeeze to
drizzle chocolate over pie.

Pictured on pages 72 and 73.

decorating with chocolate

Add a designer touch to desserts and dessert plates with a chocolate garnish,
which also will give your desserts an extra dose of rich chocolate flavor.

Grated Chocolate: Rub a solid piece of NESTLÉ TOLL HOUSE Semi-Sweet
Baking Bar across the grating section of a hand-held grater. Choose either the
fine or the large grating section to obtain the desired-size pieces.

Chocolate Curls: Carefully draw a vegetable peeler across a bar of NESTLÉ
TOLL HOUSE Semi-Sweet Chocolate. Vary the width of your curls by using
different sides of the chocolate bar.

Chocolate Dipped Fruit: Microwave 1 cup (6 ounces) morsels and
2 tablespoons shortening in microwave-safe bowl on HIGH (100%) power for
1 minute; stir. Microwave at additional 10- to 20-second intervals, stirring
until smooth. Dip fruit into chocolate mixture; shake off excess.

Chocolate Cookie Turtle Shapes

This remarkably easy recipe makes adorable cookies in the tradition of the famous chocolate TURTLES candies, which are part of the Nestlé family. They're so cute you almost hate to eat them!

2 cups (120) pecan halves	20 caramels, unwrapped
1 package (18 ounces) refrigerated NESTLÉ TOLL HOUSE Chocolate Chip Cookie Dough	2 tablespoons milk

SOAK pecans in water for 5 minutes. Arrange 5 pecans on ungreased baking sheet (1 for head, 4 for legs), leaving about a 1-inch circle in center.

SHAPE level tablespoon of cookie dough into ball; place over circle pressing onto pecans. Repeat with remaining pecans and dough, placing turtles 2 inches apart on ungreased baking sheets.

BAKE in preheated 350° F. oven for 11 to 13 minutes or until edges are crisp. Cool on baking sheets for 1 minute; remove to wire racks to cool completely.

MICROWAVE caramels and milk in microwave-safe bowl on HIGH (100%) power for 1½ minutes; stir. Microwave at additional 10-second intervals until melted. Drizzle over turtles. Makes about 2 dozen cookies.

Pictured on pages 72 and 73.

Mocha Cream Shake

The perfect union of chocolate, ice cream and coffee creates a most satisfying and smooth shake—hence the name—Mocha Cream. Enjoy.

1 pint CARNATION Vanilla Ice Cream	¼ cup NESTLÉ QUIK Real Chocolate Flavor Syrup
2 cups milk	2 tablespoons TASTER'S CHOICE Original Blend Freeze Dried Coffee

COMBINE ice cream, milk, syrup and coffee in blender container; cover. Blend on high speed for 30 seconds or just until blended. Makes 5 servings.

Pictured on pages 72 and 73.

Carnation Famous Fudge

This all-American classic recipe is a no-fail tasty treat. For variety, try using milk chocolate, butterscotch or mint-chocolate morsels instead of semi-sweet morsels.

2 tablespoons butter or margarine
⅔ cup CARNATION Evaporated Milk
1½ cups granulated sugar
¼ teaspoon salt
2 cups (4 ounces) miniature marshmallows

1½ cups (9 ounces) NESTLÉ TOLL HOUSE Semi-Sweet Chocolate Morsels
½ cup chopped pecans or walnuts
1 teaspoon vanilla extract

COMBINE butter, evaporated milk, sugar and salt in medium, heavy-duty saucepan. Bring to a *full rolling boil*, stirring constantly, over medium heat. Boil, stirring constantly, for 4 to 5 minutes. Remove from heat.

STIR in marshmallows, morsels, nuts and vanilla. Stir vigorously for 1 minute or until marshmallows are melted. Pour into foil-lined 8-inch-square baking pan; chill until firm. Makes 50 pieces.

Pictured on pages 72 and 73.

FOR MILK CHOCOLATE FUDGE:
SUBSTITUTE 2 cups (11.5-ounce package) NESTLÉ TOLL HOUSE Milk Chocolate Morsels for Semi-Sweet Morsels.

FOR BUTTERSCOTCH FUDGE:
SUBSTITUTE 1⅔ cups (11-ounce package) NESTLÉ TOLL HOUSE Butterscotch Flavored Morsels for Semi-Sweet Morsels.

FOR MINT CHOCOLATE FUDGE:
SUBSTITUTE 1½ cups (10-ounce package) NESTLÉ TOLL HOUSE Mint-Chocolate Morsels for Semi-Sweet Morsels.

Hacienda Dip (see recipe, page 81)

casual gatherings

Neighborhood Potluck

Mix-and-Match Pasta Buffet

Wine and Cheese Party

Friendly Fireside Dinner

The first day of summer, a chance to see old buddies or just for the fun of it—these are all great reasons to invite friends over for a casual meal. Choose one of these four relaxed menus, and you'll be well on your way to turning an ordinary day into a memorable one.

Neighborhood Potluck

menu

Hacienda Dip

Italian Pumpkin Strata

Stouffer's Family Size Lasagna

Grilled Hamburgers*

Antipasto Salad

Relish Platter

Chocolate Peanut Buddy Bars

Marbled Chocolate Sour Cream Cake

Nestea Suntea Style Tea

Burgundy Wine

*Prepare your favorite recipe

Although potlucks have long been a tradition, such bring-a-dish gatherings are as popular as ever today because they're perfect for busy families who want to socialize. Bring one of these simple dishes to your next potluck and include the recipe to share.

Clockwise from top right: Marbled Chocolate Sour Cream Cake (see recipe, page 83), Antipasto Salad (see recipe, page 82) and Italian Pumpkin Strata (see recipe, at right)

Hacienda Dip

Perfectly simple and incredibly satisfying, this dip is truly addictive.

1 package (8 ounces) cream cheese, softened
1½ cups (16-ounce jar) ORTEGA Thick & Chunky
Salsa, hot, medium or mild or Garden
Style Salsa, medium or mild

Chopped tomato, chopped ripe olives and
sliced green onion (optional)
Tortilla chips

BEAT cream cheese in small mixer bowl until smooth. Gradually beat in salsa.
Cover; chill for at least 2 hours. Garnish with tomato, olives and green onion. Serve
with tortilla chips. Makes 2¼ cups.

Pictured on page 79.

Italian Pumpkin Strata

*Strata can best be described as a savory version of bread pudding. This zesty sausage
strata uses pumpkin and evaporated milk to make it moist and delicious.*

1 tablespoon vegetable oil
1 pound sweet Italian sausage links,
casings removed
1 cup (1 small) chopped onion
½ cup chopped green bell pepper
½ cup chopped red bell pepper
2 cloves garlic, finely chopped
12 cups (about ¾ of a 1-pound loaf) Italian
bread or French bread, cut into
1½-inch cubes
2 cups (8 ounces) shredded mozzarella cheese

4 eggs
3 cups (*two* 12 fluid-ounce cans) CARNATION
Evaporated Milk
1¾ cups (15-ounce can) LIBBY'S Solid Pack
Pumpkin
1 teaspoon salt
½ teaspoon ground black pepper
½ teaspoon dried oregano, crushed
½ teaspoon dried basil, crushed
½ teaspoon dried marjoram, crushed

HEAT oil in large skillet over medium-high heat. Add sausage, onion, bell peppers
and garlic. Cook, stirring to break up sausage, for 7 to 10 minutes or until sausage is
no longer pink; drain.

COMBINE bread cubes, cheese and sausage mixture in large bowl.

BEAT eggs, evaporated milk, pumpkin, salt, pepper, oregano, basil and marjoram in
medium bowl. Pour over bread mixture, pressing bread into egg mixture. Pour into
13 x 9-inch baking pan.

BAKE in preheated 350° F. oven for 30 to 35 minutes or until set. Serve warm.
Makes 12 servings.

Antipasto Salad

*A vivid combination of colors, tastes and textures complements each other
to make this popular Italian favorite.*

6 cups (16-ounce package) dried rotini or
    rotelle pasta, cooked, drained and chilled
1¾ cups (14.5-ounce can) CONTADINA Pasta
    Ready Chunky Tomatoes with Olive Oil,
    Garlic and Spices, undrained
1 cup prepared Italian salad dressing
1 cup (1 small) sliced red bell pepper
1 cup (1 small) sliced green bell pepper

1 cup (4 ounces) cubed mozzarella cheese
1 cup (4 ounces) cubed or sliced salami or
    pepperoni
½ cup pitted ripe olives, halved
½ cup sliced pepperoncini
½ cup sliced marinated artichoke hearts
½ cup chopped fresh basil (optional)

COMBINE pasta, tomatoes and juice, salad dressing, bell peppers, cheese, salami,
olives, pepperoncini, artichoke hearts and basil in large bowl. Toss well to coat.

COVER; chill for at least 2 hours or overnight. Makes 8 to 10 servings.

Pictured on page 80.

Chocolate Peanut Buddy Bars

*One of our most requested recipes, these quick-fix bars feature the ever-popular
combination of chocolate and peanut butter that makes them a winner every time.*

1 cup creamy or chunky peanut butter
6 tablespoons butter or margarine, softened
1¼ cups granulated sugar
3 eggs
1 teaspoon vanilla extract

1 cup all-purpose flour
¼ teaspoon salt
2 cups (11.5-ounce package)
    NESTLÉ TOLL HOUSE Milk Chocolate
    Morsels, *divided*

BEAT peanut butter and butter in large mixer bowl until smooth. Beat in sugar, eggs
and vanilla. Beat in flour and salt. Stir in *1 cup* morsels. Spread into ungreased
13 x 9-inch baking pan.

BAKE in preheated 350° F. oven for 25 to 30 minutes or until edges are lightly
browned. Immediately sprinkle with *remaining* morsels. Let stand for 5 minutes or
until morsels are shiny and soft; spread evenly. Cool completely in pan on wire rack.
Makes 3 dozen bars.

Marbled Chocolate Sour Cream Cake

The pretty chocolate swirl running through the cake and the moist rich flavor
of this mouth-watering recipe make this cake a legend in its own time.

1 cup (6 ounces) NESTLÉ TOLL HOUSE Semi-
   Sweet Chocolate Morsels
1 package (18.5 ounces) yellow cake mix
4 eggs
¾ cup sour cream

½ cup vegetable oil
¼ cup water
¼ cup granulated sugar
   Powdered sugar (optional)

MICROWAVE morsels in medium, microwave-safe bowl on HIGH (100%)
power for 1 minute; stir. Microwave at additional 10- to 20-second intervals, stirring
until smooth.

COMBINE cake mix, eggs, sour cream, oil, water and granulated sugar in large
mixer bowl. Beat on low speed until moistened. Beat on high speed for 2 minutes.

STIR 2 cups batter into melted chocolate. Alternately spoon batters into greased
10-cup bundt or round tube pan.

BAKE in preheated 375° F. oven for 35 to 45 minutes or until wooden pick inserted
in center comes out clean. Cool in pan for 20 minutes; invert onto wire rack to cool
completely. Sprinkle with powdered sugar before serving. Makes 24 servings.

Pictured on page 80.

menu

Hot and Spicy Sausage Sauce

Roasted Vegetable Pesto Sauce

Refrigerated Contadina Alfredo
or Four Cheese Sauce

Refrigerated Contadina Fettuccine
or Linguine

Crusty Italian Bread

Cabernet Sauvignon Wine

Mocha Bread Pudding with
Caramel Sauce

Carnation Hot Cocoa

*Clockwise from top right: refrigerated Contadina Fettuccine, refrigerated Contadina Alfredo Sauce, (next two bowls) Roas
Vegetable Pesto Sauce (see recipe, page 86) and Hot and Spicy Sausage Sauce (see recipe, at rig*

Mix-and-Match
Pasta Buffet

People's taste preferences come in all shapes and sizes—and
thankfully, pasta does, too. Let your guests serve themselves by
customizing their pasta with either of these savory sauces, both easy
enough for last-minute or weeknight entertaining.

Hot and Spicy Sausage Sauce

This extremely easy-to-make hearty sauce uses only four ingredients.
Freeze any leftovers for another evening.

1 tablespoon olive oil
1 pound mild Italian sausage links,
   casings removed
2 cups (2 small) sliced green or
   red bell peppers

3½ cups (*two* 14-ounce cans) CONTADINA Pasta
   Ready Chunky Tomatoes with Spicy Red
   Pepper, undrained
   Hot cooked pasta

HEAT oil in large skillet over medium-high heat. Add sausage; cook, stirring to
break into small pieces, for 5 to 10 minutes or until no longer pink. Drain, reserving
1 tablespoon oil in skillet.

ADD bell peppers to skillet. Reduce heat to medium; cook for 2 to 4 minutes or
until crisp-tender. Stir in tomatoes and juice. Reduce heat to low; cook for 5 to
7 minutes to develop flavor. Serve over pasta. Makes 8 to 12 servings.

Roasted Vegetable Pesto Sauce

This robust sauce is a spirited addition to any buffet. The use of two ready-made products such as the tomatoes and the pesto makes this recipe a real time-saver.

1⅓ cups (*two* 7-ounce containers) refrigerated CONTADINA Pesto with Sun Dried Tomatoes, warmed
1 medium eggplant, cut into ½-inch-thick slices
1 *each* red, yellow and green bell pepper, halved
1½ cups (2 small) sliced zucchini
8 ounces fresh mushrooms

1 medium onion, quartered
3 cloves garlic, peeled
1¾ cups (14.5-ounce can) CONTADINA Pasta Ready Chunky Tomatoes with Olive Oil, Garlic and Spices, undrained
Hot cooked pasta

SPOON oil off top of pesto into small bowl; reserve. Place eggplant, bell peppers, zucchini, mushrooms, onion and garlic in single layer on two 15 x 10-inch jelly-roll pans. Brush with pesto oil.

BAKE in preheated 450° F. oven for about 20 minutes or until vegetables are tender. Coarsely chop into ½- to ¾-inch pieces. Mix vegetables, tomatoes and juice and pesto in large bowl. Serve warm over pasta. Makes 8 to 12 servings.

Pictured on page 84.

fresh pasta pointers

Fresh tasting and easy to prepare, refrigerated pastas make a convenient dinner option for weeknights and entertaining. CONTADINA refrigerated pastas come in a variety of shapes and exciting flavors and only take one to eight minutes to cook. When preparing refrigerated pasta, consider the following tips:

• Refrigerated pasta contains more moisture than dried pasta and cooks faster, so be careful not to overcook. Use the cooking time on the package as a guide, but also test the pasta. Pasta should be cooked until al dente, which means that the pasta should have a somewhat firm texture and should be slightly chewy. Overcooked pasta turns limp and sticky.

• It's unnecessary to rinse pasta after cooking if serving it hot. For cold pasta salads, however, rinse the pasta with cool water to keep it from sticking together.

• Cooked pasta can be stored in an airtight container in the refrigerator for up to four days. Before storing, rinse with cold water and toss with a little oil. To reheat, immerse pasta in a pot of boiling water just until warmed, then drain.

• For added flavor, cook pasta in boiling water with a little fresh lemon or orange juice.

Mocha Bread Pudding with Caramel Sauce

This impressive pudding is delicious served warm from the oven when the edges become toasty chocolate bites. This may be made a day ahead—simply reheat in the oven and serve with whipped cream or vanilla ice cream, if desired.

9 cups (about ¾ of a 1-pound loaf) French bread, cut into 1-inch cubes
1 cup granulated sugar
¼ cup NESTLÉ TOLL HOUSE Baking Cocoa
1 tablespoon TASTER'S CHOICE Original Blend Freeze Dried Coffee

4 eggs
3 cups (*two* 12 fluid-ounce cans) CARNATION Evaporated Skimmed Milk or Evaporated Lowfat Milk, *divided*
2 teaspoons vanilla extract
Caramel Sauce (recipe follows)

PLACE bread cubes in greased 2-quart baking dish. Combine sugar, cocoa and coffee granules in small bowl.

BEAT eggs, *2⅔ cups* evaporated milk and vanilla in medium bowl until well blended; stir in sugar mixture. Pour over bread, pressing bread into milk mixture.

BAKE in preheated 350° F. oven for 50 to 55 minutes or until set. Serve warm with Caramel Sauce. Makes 12 servings.

FOR CARAMEL SAUCE:
COMBINE ⅔ cup packed brown sugar, ¼ cup (½ stick) butter or margarine and 1 tablespoon light corn syrup in small saucepan. Cook, stirring constantly, over medium-low heat for 2 to 3 minutes or until sugar is dissolved. Slowly stir in *remaining* evaporated milk. Bring to a boil, stirring constantly; cook for 1 minute. Remove from heat. Serve warm.

Wine and Cheese Party

There's no better way to welcome the weekend than to gather with friends on a Friday evening for a glass of wine and good conversation. These hearty appetizers are perfect accompaniments to both—and they can be partially assembled or made ahead so they're virtually ready and waiting when you get home.

Polenta Primavera

A twist on the classic Italian staple made of cornmeal, this polenta dish incorporates two cheeses, cream and tomatoes for an extra-rich flavor.

2 cups water
⅔ cup ALBERS Yellow Corn Meal
1 cup (4 ounces) shredded fontina or mozzarella cheese
½ cup heavy whipping cream
¼ cup (1 ounce) grated Parmesan cheese

½ teaspoon salt
¼ teaspoon ground black pepper
1¾ cups (14-ounce can) CONTADINA Pasta Ready Chunky Tomatoes, Primavera, undrained

BRING water to a boil in medium saucepan. Slowly add cornmeal, stirring constantly, over medium heat for 2 to 3 minutes or until slightly thick.

STIR in fontina cheese, cream, Parmesan cheese, salt and pepper; cook, stirring constantly, for an additional 2 minutes or until very thick.

SPREAD into greased 9-inch pie plate; cool for 1 hour or until firm. Cut into wedges; serve topped with tomatoes and juice. Makes 8 appetizer servings.

menu

Polenta Primavera

Bundle of Brie with Apple Slices

Chile and Cheese Spirals

Cheese Wedges, Grapes and Pears

Pinot Noir Wine

On plate left to right: Chile and Cheese Spirals (see recipe, page 91) and Polenta Primavera (see recipe, at left)
Background: Bundle of Brie (see recipe, page 90)

Bundle of Brie

Wrapped like a present with layers of crisp pastry, this creamy Brie appetizer is surprisingly easy to make. To preserve freshness while assembling, cover the filo dough with plastic wrap and then a damp towel.

4 sheets filo dough
⅔ cup (7-ounce container) refrigerated
    CONTADINA Pesto with Basil

1 8-ounce wheel Brie cheese
    Apple and pear slices

BRUSH each sheet of filo dough with oil from top of pesto, stacking them on top of each other on ungreased baking sheet. Center cheese on top of filo sheets. Gather filo up around cheese. Lightly press filo against sides and top of cheese so excess filo forms a sunburst on top. Lightly brush outside with pesto oil.

BAKE in preheated 375° F. oven for 20 to 25 minutes or until golden brown. Pull top open with fork. Break apart filo. Use filo pieces, apples and pears for dipping. Serve with remaining pesto, if desired. Makes 16 appetizer servings.

Pictured on page 89.

at-a-glance wine guide

Wine adds a richness to gatherings, especially around the holiday season. To help you select wine for your next gathering, here is a quick guide. Follow these pointers and your party will take off with a resounding pop of the cork:

• Shop at stores that have a knowledgeable staff. Before you go, know how much money you want to spend and what your menu is, then ask a salesperson for help in selecting the wine.
• Before buying a large quantity of wine, taste it. Many wine stores will open a bottle for sampling. If not, buy one bottle first and try it. Wine is typically less expensive by the case.
• A good way to keep track of wines you like is to keep a wine journal. Every time you sample a wine you like at home or in a restaurant, jot down the name of the grape variety (such as Chardonnay), winery, vintage and cost.

Chile and Cheese Spirals

Resembling pinwheels, this easy-to-make hors d'oeuvre combines the creamy texture of cheese and the mildly hot flavor of chiles to create a perfect complement to your favorite wine.

4 ounces cream cheese, softened
1 cup (4 ounces) shredded cheddar cheese
½ cup (4-ounce can) ORTEGA Diced Green
    Chiles
½ cup (about 6) sliced green onions

½ cup (2¼-ounce can) chopped ripe olives
4 (8-inch) soft taco-size flour tortillas
    ORTEGA Garden Style Salsa, medium or
    mild (optional)

COMBINE cream cheese, cheddar cheese, chiles, green onions and olives in medium bowl.

SPREAD ½ cup cheese mixture on each tortilla. Roll up. Wrap each roll in plastic wrap; chill for 1 hour.

REMOVE plastic wrap; slice each roll into six ¾-inch pieces. Serve with salsa for dipping. Makes 24 appetizer servings.

Pictured on page 89.

- When purchasing wine, keep in mind that one 750-ml bottle roughly serves four to five glasses. A simple rule of thumb is to plan one bottle for every two to three guests. Any unopened bottles can always be saved for later.
- With an appetizer buffet, consider serving two or three different wines. This takes into account the variety of foods and your guests' wine preferences.
- When serving several wines throughout a meal, start with the most delicately flavored wine (usually a white, such as Chenin Blanc, or a Rosé) and end with the most full-bodied wine (such as Cabernet Sauvignon or Merlot).
- Serve white wines slightly chilled. Refrigerate an unopened bottle for one or two hours or immerse for 20 minutes in an ice bucket filled with ice and a little water.
- To get the full flavor from most red wines, serve them at a cool room temperature (about 65° F.).

menu

Hearty Beef Stew

Italian-Style Salad

Crusty Rolls

Arrowhead Mountain Spring Water

Chocolate Marshmallow
Mile-High Squares

MJB European Roast Coffee

Hearty Beef Stew (see recipe, at right) and Italian-Style Salad (see recipe, page 94)

Friendly Fireside
Dinner

No invitations are needed for this inviting fireside scene. Just right

for after cold-weather fun or simply the spur-of-the-moment, a bowl

of comforting stew takes the chill off of a brisk winter's night. Our

fudgy mile-high squares and coffee add the perfect finishing touches.

Hearty Beef Stew

A Nestlé favorite, serve this traditional stew with warm crusty bread for a satisfying meal. Prepare this a day ahead and chill overnight for heightened flavor.

¼ cup all-purpose flour
1 teaspoon salt
¼ teaspoon ground black pepper
2 pounds beef stew meat, cut into 2-inch pieces
¼ cup vegetable oil
1 cup (1 small) chopped onion
1 cup (2 stalks) coarsely chopped celery
3 cloves garlic, finely chopped
4 cups (2 large) peeled, coarsely chopped potatoes

3½ cups (28-ounce can) CONTADINA Crushed Tomatoes
2 cups (about 3 large) peeled, coarsely chopped carrots
1½ cups water
1 MAGGI Beef Bouillon Tablet or 2 MAGGI Beef Bouillon Cubes
½ teaspoon ground thyme
Thyme sprigs (optional)

COMBINE flour, salt and pepper in medium bowl. Add meat; toss well to coat.

HEAT oil in large saucepan over medium-high heat. Add meat, onion, celery and garlic. Cook, stirring frequently, for 6 to 8 minutes or until meat is no longer pink and vegetables are tender.

ADD potatoes, crushed tomatoes, carrots, water, bouillon and ground thyme. Bring to a boil. Reduce heat to low; cover. Cook, stirring occasionally, for 45 to 60 minutes or until vegetables and meat are tender. Garnish with thyme sprigs. Makes 12 servings.

Italian-Style Salad

*Tangy and not sweet, the dressing on this salad offers a
fresh taste alternative to bottled dressings.*

¾ cup olive oil
⅔ cup (6-ounce can) CONTADINA Tomato Paste
½ cup water
⅓ cup red wine vinegar
¼ cup (1 ounce) grated Parmesan cheese

2 tablespoons granulated sugar
1 tablespoon dried minced onion
1 teaspoon garlic salt
1 teaspoon dried oregano, crushed
16 cups torn mixed lettuce, chilled

COMBINE oil, tomato paste, water, vinegar, cheese, sugar, onion, garlic salt and
oregano in blender container; cover. Blend thoroughly; chill. Toss with lettuce just
before serving. Makes 12 to 14 servings.

Pictured on page 92.

Chocolate Marshmallow Mile-High Squares

*Marshmallows give this no-bake fudgy treat an airy appeal, making it
all the more tempting—a true time-saver and crowd-pleaser!*

2 cups (12-ounce package) NESTLÉ TOLL
HOUSE Semi-Sweet Chocolate Morsels
1⅔ cups (11-ounce package) NESTLÉ TOLL
HOUSE Butterscotch Flavored Morsels

½ cup creamy or chunky peanut butter
9 cups (16-ounce package) miniature
marshmallows
1 cup dry roasted peanuts

MICROWAVE semi-sweet morsels, butterscotch morsels and peanut butter in large,
microwave-safe bowl on MEDIUM-HIGH (70%) power for 2 minutes; stir.
Microwave at additional 10- to 20-second intervals, stirring until smooth. Cool for
1 minute. Stir in marshmallows and nuts.

SPREAD into foil-lined 13 x 9-inch baking pan. Chill until firm. Makes 48 squares.

Index

Antipasto Salad......................82

Appetizers
Breaded Ravioli with
    Dipping Sauces..............33
Bruschetta with Capers
    and Olives 22
Bundle of Brie 90
Chile and Cheese Spirals....91
Mini Corn Quiches 22
Polenta Primavera..............88
Savory Pumpkin
    Cheese Ball 34
Thai Pumpkin Satay 21

BBQ Chicken with
    Spicy Marinade 49
Berry Banana Smoothie 42

Beverages
Berry Banana Smoothie 42
Chocolate Eggnog..............19
Mocha Cream Shake..........77
Nectar Sparkler 42

Breaded Ravioli
    with Dipping Sauces 33

Breads
Fiesta Corn Bread..............69
Garlic Toast 60
Orange Brunch Muffins......42
Pumpkin Blueberry
    Streusel Muffins.............43
Pumpkin Corn Muffins.......26
Southwestern Biscuits 49

Brisket with Caramelized
    Onion Sauce......................30
Bruschetta with Capers
    and Olives 22
Bundle of Brie 90
Butterscotch Fudge 78

Candies
Butterscotch Fudge............78
Carnation Famous Fudge ...78
Chocolate Chip Party Mix...39

Candies (cont.)
Chocolate Marshmallow
    Mile-High Squares 94
Milk Chocolate Fudge.........78
Mint Chocolate Fudge.......78

Candy Shop Pizza 67
Caramel Sauce 87
Carnation Famous Fudge 78
Cheddar Potato Soup.............27
Cheesy Macaroni
    and Hot Dogs....................54
Chicken and Wild Rice Soup....26
Chile and Cheese Spirals........91
Chocolate Chip Fruit Tart.......47
Chocolate Chip Party Mix.......39
Chocolate Cookie
    Turtle Shapes 77
Chocolate Crinkle-Top
    Cookies 19
Chocolate Drizzle 76
Chocolate Eggnog.................19
Chocolate Marshmallow
    Mile-High Squares 94
Chocolate Peanut
    Buddy Bars 82
Chutney Salsa 23

Cookies
Chocolate Cookie
    Turtle Shapes 77
Chocolate Crinkle-Top
    Cookies 19
Chocolate Peanut
    Buddy Bars 82
Extra-Easy Cut-Out
    Cookies 18
Fudgy Caramel Brownies ...23
Lemon Bars 17
Monster Pops 56
Original Nestlé Toll House
    Chocolate Chip Cookies...16
Original Nestlé Toll House
    Chocolate Chip
    Pan Cookies 16
Original Nestlé Toll House
    Chocolate Chip Slice-
    and-Bake Cookies 16

Cookies (cont.)
Pumpkin White Chip
    Macadamia Bars 18
Star of David Chocolate
    Cookies 31

Corn Pudding 9
Cream Cheese Crab Dip 46
Cream of Pumpkin
    Curry Soup.......................60
Creamy Gazpacho 46
Creamy Pesto
    Dipping Sauce....................9

Desserts
Candy Shop Pizza 67
Chocolate Chip
    Fruit Tart 47
Glazed Chocolate
    Sweet Cakes...................75
Luscious Chocolate
    Mousse Pie 76
Marbled Chocolate
    Sour Cream Cake 83
Mini Cream
    Cheese Flans..................71
Mocha Bread Pudding
    with Caramel Sauce 87
Pumpkin Pecan Pie...........13
Rich Chocolate
    Mocha Mousse 63
Spiderweb Munch.............54
Summer Berry
    Brownie Torte................50
Tuxedo Cheesecake...........74

Dips
Chutney Salsa 23
Cream Cheese Crab Dip 46
Creamy Pesto
    Dipping Sauce.................9
Hacienda Dip....................81
Layered Sombrero Dip.......36
Ortega Guacamole.............71
Warm Spinach Dip
    in a Bread Bowl.............34

Easy Apple Cranberry Relish.....11

English Muffin Pizzas.............52
Extra-Easy Cut-Out Cookies ...18
Fiesta Corn Bread..................69
Fiesta Pizza 66
Firecracker Pasta Salad.........50
Fudgy Caramel Brownies 23
Garlic Rosemary
    Mashed Potatoes 11
Garlic Toast..........................60
Glazed Chocolate
    Sweet Cakes......................75
Hacienda Dip.........................81
Hearty Beef Stew...................93
Hot and Spicy Sausage Sauce....85
Italian Pumpkin Strata...........81
Italian Quiche 41
Italian-Style Salad 94
Juicy Gelatin Salad................65
Layered Sombrero Dip...........36
Lemon Bars 17
Luscious Chocolate
    Mousse Pie 76

Main Dishes

BBQ Chicken with Spicy
    Marinade........................49
Brisket with Caramelized
    Onion Sauce...................30
Cheddar Potato Soup.........27
Cheesy Macaroni
    and Hot Dogs.................54
Chicken and Wild
    Rice Soup 26
English Muffin Pizzas.........52
Fiesta Pizza 66
Hearty Beef Stew...............93
Italian Pumpkin Strata.......81
Italian Quiche 41
Minestrone.........................27
Nacho Pizza 65
Poached Salmon with
    Four Cheese Sauce 61
Pumpkin Chili Mexicana.....38

Marbled Chocolate Sour
    Cream Cake......................83
Mexican Rice........................70
Milk Chocolate Fudge...........78
Minestrone...........................27
Mini Corn Quiches................22
Mini Cream Cheese Flans......71
Mint Chocolate Fudge 78

Mocha Bread Pudding
    with Caramel Sauce 87
Mocha Cream Shake..............77
Monster Pops 56
Nacho Pizza 65
Nectar Sparkler.....................42
Orange Brunch Muffins..........42
Original Nestlé Toll House
    Chocolate Chip Cookies.......16
Original Nestlé Toll House
    Chocolate Chip
    Pan Cookies 16
Original Nestlé Toll House
    Chocolate Chip Slice-
    and-Bake Cookies 16
Ortega Guacamole.................71

Pizzas

English Muffin Pizzas.........52
Fiesta Pizza 66
Nacho Pizza 65

Poached Salmon
    with Four Cheese Sauce.....61
Polenta Primavera.................88
Potato Latkes 31
Pumpkin Blueberry
    Streusel Muffins................43
Pumpkin Chili Mexicana.........38
Pumpkin Corn Muffins...........26
Pumpkin Pecan Pie 13
Pumpkin White Chip
    Macadamia Bars 18
Rich Chocolate Mocha Mousse..63
Roasted Vegetable
    Pesto Sauce 86

Salads

Antipasto Salad 82
Firecracker Pasta Salad......50
Italian-Style Salad 94
Juicy Gelatin Salad.............65
Warm Ravioli Pear Salad ...47

Sauces

Caramel Sauce 87
Easy Apple
    Cranberry Relish 11
Hot and Spicy
    Sausage Sauce.............85
Roasted Vegetable
    Pesto Sauce 86

Savory Pumpkin
    Cheese Ball 34

Soups

Cheddar Potato Soup.........27
Chicken and Wild
    Rice Soup 26
Cream of Pumpkin
    Curry Soup.....................60
Creamy Gazpacho 46
Hearty Beef Stew...............93
Minestrone.........................27
Pumpkin Chili
    Mexicana.......................38
Sweet and Tangy
    Cabbage Soup...............29

Southwestern Biscuits 49
Spiderweb Munch 54
Star of David
    Chocolate Cookies 31
Summer Berry
    Brownie Torte....................50
Sweet and Tangy
    Cabbage Soup...................29
Thai Pumpkin Satay 21
Tuxedo Cheesecake...............74
Warm Ravioli Pear Salad 47
Warm Spinach Dip
    in a Bread Bowl.................34

TIP INDEX

At-a-Glance Wine Guide....90-91
Chocolate Eggnog.................19
Chocolate Zigzags.................63
Choice Cheesecakes..............74
Coffee Bar 13
Decorating with Chocolate 76
Extra-Easy
    Cut-Out Cookies................18
Fresh Pasta Pointers.............86
Fruity Breakfast Sippers........42
Game Plan for Victory...........39
Garlic Toast..........................60
Ice-Cream
    Dream Sundaes 66
Taco Bar...............................70
Turkey Roasting Guide..........10

96